ADDISON WESLEY LONGMAN HISTORY IN DEPTH SERIES

CHARLES I
and the causes of the seventeenth-century crisis

Angela Anderson
Series editor: Christopher Culpin

D0532319

CONTENTS

INTRODUCTION

The popular view of King Charles I can be summarised in the cartoon overleaf – an ineffective king who quarrelled with parliament, provoked Civil War, refused to come to terms with defeat, and finally had to be removed from the throne by having his head removed from his shoulders, which created a crisis in English government.

While historians disagree radically about the causes of this crisis, there is widespread agreement that Charles was partly responsible for it and, at the very least, inept in his handling of the situation. Variously described as 'untrustworthy' (Conrad Russell), 'authoritarian' (John Morrill) and 'psychologically incapable of dealing with a parliament that was anything more than a rubber stamp' (Charles Carlton), Charles's personality is so obviously a cause of the war that it becomes hard to explain why he was able to raise an army to fight for him.

The fact that he did raise an army, and that he was later mourned as a martyr, suggests that the cartoon is an over-simplification. To understand the part that he played in these events we need not only to study Charles's personality and beliefs more fully, but to weigh them against other factors – the actions of his opponents, the attitudes and beliefs of the period, and the problems that he inherited.

Historians' interpretations

The events of these years were portrayed by contemporaries as arising largely from individual actions and personalities – as a struggle for liberty against a tyrannical king, or for order against rebellious factions and religious fanatics. However, later historians emphasised underlying structural problems as the cause of revolution, or at least of a seventeenth-century crisis.

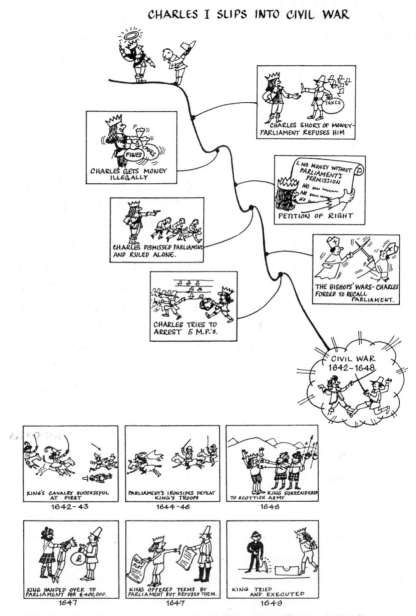

Figure 1 School textbook cartoon showing how England 'slipped into civil war' under King Charles I.

Debate focused on the causes of the crisis – religious and political, social and economic – and on its scope as an English, British or European experience. There is little sign of an overall consensus. Indeed, in recent years some historians have tended to challenge the whole idea of a structural crisis, and to re-emphasise the influence of individuals.

The argument in favour of a structural crisis of some kind is strengthened by the study of European governments in this period. The mid-seventeenth century saw rebellions in Britain, France, Spain, Italy, Portugal and the Dutch Republic, as well as a civil war in Germany. There is some evidence to suggest that they arose from common causes. In the sixteenth century a rapid increase in population created land hunger and inflation. The Protestant reformation and the resulting religious problems led to war both within and between states, and war created new demands on government for the efficient exploitation of resources. Everywhere, governments sought to increase central control, to raise new taxes, and to reduce local or factional independence in the interests of efficiency. Inevitably, this led to strains and tensions, and often to violent resistance.

This pattern of development applied in Britain as in other parts of Europe. In 1603 King James VI of Scotland became king of England, Wales and Ireland. This would inevitably require some review and redefinition of the relationship between the British kingdoms, with pressure for greater uniformity of government. The process was further complicated by the religious divisions which cut across all three kingdoms. Moreover, James inherited a crown which was facing financial problems arising from inflation and a long war against Spain, and whose administration depended on the services of an unpaid ruling class and their representatives in parliament.

Defining the issues

It is clear that problems and tensions existed within the system of government before Charles I became king. Whether or not these problems need have amounted to a crisis is more debatable. By 1642 there was civil war throughout Britain, leading to the trial and execution of the monarch for treason. Monarchy was abolished, along with the House of Lords, in 1649. Eleven years later, it was restored without prior conditions, but problems soon re-emerged, resulting in a new 'revolution' in 1688, in which fundamental reforms were established.

The purpose of this book is to examine the role of Charles I in creating this crisis, and to raise some issues regarding its nature and development. The first task can be approached by considering three questions.

◢ **What problems existed within the structure of government when Charles I became king in 1625?**
◢ **What actions did Charles take to deal with them?**
◢ **How did these two factors interact to bring about a crisis and civil war by 1642?**

The answers produced by these will then allow some conclusions to be drawn as to the significance of Charles, as *an individual*, in creating the crisis of 1642. It is also clear, however, that the crisis was not resolved by the war, nor by Charles's death.

This may imply that the structural problems were too serious to be resolved so easily, and therefore that they were more significant in causing the crisis than the actions of Charles as an individual. Although these issues cannot fully be resolved in a book of this size, they can be considered and used to identify further areas to study and explore.

Chronology

1625   Accession of Charles 1
1626   William Laud appointed Bishop of Bath and Wells
1627   Five Knights' Case; forced loans declared to be legal
1628   Petition of Right
Assassination of Buckingham
Sir Thomas Wentworth appointed President of the Council of the North; Laud appointed Bishop of London
1629   The Three Resolutions and Dissolution of Parliament
1632   Wentworth appointed Lord Deputy of Ireland
1633   Laud becomes Archbishop of Canterbury
1634   Ship-money levied
1635   Ship-money levied and extended to inland areas
1637   Hampden Case; judges found for the King by 5 to 3
1638   The Scots enter a National Covenant for the defence of their religion
1639   First Bishops' War, ending in the Treaty of Berwick
1640   Scottish Synod vote to abolish the Prayer Book and Bishops
Sir Thomas Wentworth created Lord Strafford and the King's main adviser
Short Parliament called (April); dissolved in May
Laudian 'Canons' (codifying and enforcing Laudian reforms in the English Church) published in June
Second Bishops' War (June–Oct.), ending in Treaty of Ripon
Long Parliament meets (November); begins impeachment of Laud and Strafford
Laudian Canons declared illegal
Laud imprisoned in the Tower of London (Dec.)
1641   Bishops dismissed from political office (Jan.)
Triennial Act passed (Feb.)
First Army Plot (March); revealed to Commons (3 May)
Attainder Act against Strafford introduced (April)
Bishops' Exclusion Bill sent to Lords (1 May)
Strafford's Attainder signed by the King (10 May)
Act against Dissolution of Parliament without its consent (10 May)
Execution of Strafford (12 May)
Root and Branch Bill debated in the Commons; laid aside on 27 May
Lords rejected the Bishops' Exclusion Bill (8 June)
Ten Propositions presented to the King (24 June)
Acts abolishing the Prerogative Courts (July)
Ship-money declared illegal (August)
King leaves to visit Scotland (13 August)
Irish rebellion breaks out (23 Oct.)
Grand Remonstrance (Nov.); printed and published 15 Dec.

1642 King's attempt to arrest the five MPs (4 Jan.)
King leaves London (10 Jan.)
Bishops excluded from the House of Lords (Feb.)
The queen sails to seek military help in Holland and France (13 Feb.)
Militia Ordinance passed by parliament (5 March)
King denied entrance to Hull (23 April)
The Nineteen Propositions sent from parliament to King (June)
Parliament establishes a Committee of Safety (4 July) and votes to raise an army
The King raises his standard at Nottingham (22 August)
Battle of Edgehill; King able to move towards London (Oct.)
Royal forces stopped at Battle of Turnham Green; King retreats to winter in Oxford

1643 Peace negotiations at Oxford fail (May)
Solemn League and Covenant (alliance) concluded between parliament and Scots
Death of John Pym (Dec.)

1644 Parliamentary victory at Marston Moor (June)

1645 Formation of New Model Army (Jan.–March)
Battle of Naseby; military and political disaster for the King (June)

1646 King leaves Oxford and surrenders to the Scots (April)
Surrender of Oxford marks virtual end of the war (June)
Peace terms offered to the King at Newcastle (July)

1647 Scots hand King to parliament and leave England (Feb.)
Parliament votes for disbandment of the Army (April)
Regiments refuse to disband on 31 May
Seizure of the King by Cornet Joyce (4 June)
Heads of the Proposals presented to the King (2 August)
The King signs an Engagement inviting the Scots to invade England (Dec.)

1648 Parliament votes 'No Further Addresses' to the King (Jan.)
Risings in Kent, Essex, Cornwall, Yorkshire and South Wales (April); easily dealt
with except at Colchester (Essex) and in Wales. Scottish army led by royalist
Scots enters England (July); Cromwell completes defeat of Welsh rising and
catches the Scots at Preston (17 August)
Colchester forced to surrender to Fairfax – end of Second Civil War (Sept.).
Parliamentary commissioners sent to renew negotiations with the King
Army Remonstrance demands the trial and punishment of the King (Nov.)
House of Commons votes the King's reply to their commissioners to be the basis
for negotiations (5 Dec.)
Pride's Purge (6 Dec.)

1649 High Court of Justice set up to try the King (1 Jan.)
The King's trial opens (20 Jan.); King Charles executed (30 Jan.)
Abolition of the Monarchy and House of Lords (March).

PART ONE

SEVENTEENTH-CENTURY ENGLAND

Government and social structure

Charles I came to the throne in 1625, inheriting a system of government which had evolved through a century of Tudor rule and the reign of his father, James I. The following pages set out the main features of this government, and of the social structure that supported it. The two are described together because they were mutually dependent – a threat to one was a threat to both; it is impossible to understand the nature and outcome of the mid-seventeenth-century crisis unless this fact is appreciated.

The social structure

Society was seen as a hierarchy, with a number of parallel strands and the King at its head. Although there were ranks and divisions within the nobility and gentry, the key distinction lay between the gentry, who governed, and those below them, who did not. Economic development and expanding trade had created a measure of social mobility within the hierarchy, and it was possible for wealthy merchants and yeomen to move into the ranks of the gentry by buying landed estates and educating or marrying off their children appropriately. In addition, the younger sons of gentry, who did not inherit large estates, might well enter trade or one of the professions. These, however, were individual movements, which might blur the edges, but did not significantly change the structure of the social ladder or its relationship to government (see Figure 2 overleaf).

National government

Power in government centred upon the King but was exercised through a variety of institutions. The Royal Court, a combination of the King's household and office, was both a social and political institution. It housed the king's family, friends and associates, but because it gave access to the king, it was also a magnet for those with political interests and ambitions and those involved in government institutions. The most important of these were the Church, and the Privy Council, both directly controlled by the King.

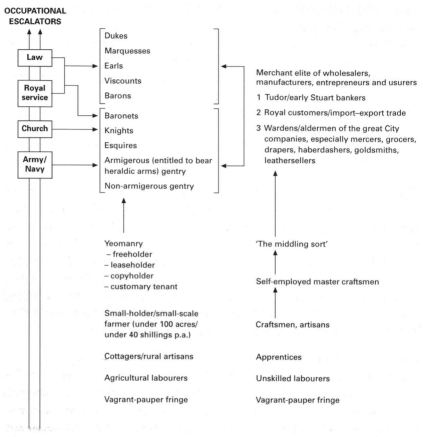

OCCUPATIONAL ESCALATORS

Figure 2 A model of the social structure of sixteenth- and seventeenth-century England and Wales (source: taken from M. A. R. Graves and R. H. Silcock *Revolution, Reaction and the Triumph of Conservatism*, Longman Paul, 1984)

The Reformation of the 1530s had brought the Church under the control of the monarchy, enhancing the King's claims to divine status and providing a propaganda machine that reached into every town and village. The Church taught obedience and respect for the social hierarchy and reinforced the authority of government, both central and local.

The Privy Council provided the main channel for the exercise of that authority. Privy Councillors were appointed and dismissed by the king, and exercised authority in his name. The Privy Council appointed and supervised local magistrates, provided central administration, and staffed the Prerogative Courts of Chancery, Star Chamber, High Commission and the regional Councils of the North and Welsh Marches. The key feature of all these bodies was that they exercised power directly from the king. The Court of Chancery dealt with wills and civil matters, High Commission covered religion and the Church, while Star Chamber and the regional councils had been developed to assert royal power in all parts and at all levels of society. They were respected for their speed and clear decisions, but disliked when they overruled local concerns in the interests of the King.

These local interests functioned in a system of local government based on Justices of the Peace (JPs) and the Common Law, which was a mixture of custom, precedent, royal charters and statutes made in parliament. The central Common Law Courts were in London and the regional Assize Courts were held by judges chosen by the king, but the JPs ran local Petty and Quarter Sessions to deal with both minor crime and administrative matters. In addition, local interests were expressed and represented through the occasional meetings of Parliament. The structure of government is summarised in Figure 3 overleaf.

Local government and the governing class

These arrangements reflect the integration of government and the social structure through the role and functions of the ruling class. This was a county elite of nobility and gentry, known to one another socially, linked by ties of blood and marriage, who made up the social and political leadership of the region and jealously guarded their right to govern it. They were supported by merchant elites in the corporate boroughs (self-governing towns) that lay within the county, who acted as mayors and aldermen. At their head was a Lord Lieutenant of the county, appointed by the King and Privy Council, but drawn from the local nobility. The Lord Lieutenant represented local needs and opinions in central government circles. He was supported by a number of Deputy-Lieutenants, who could often exercise considerable influence in the local community, especially if the Lord Lieutenant was inactive or frequently absent. As the agent of central government, the Lord Lieutenant advised on the appointment of Justices of the Peace. They were unpaid but the position conferred considerable status and was therefore highly prized among the gentry.

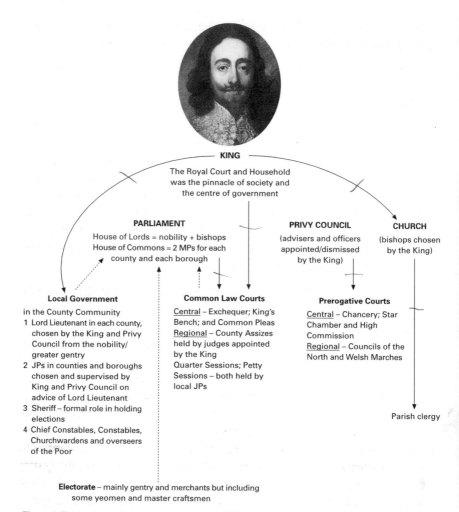

KING

The Royal Court and Household was the pinnacle of society and the centre of government

PARLIAMENT

House of Lords = nobility + bishops
House of Commons = 2 MPs for each county and each borough

PRIVY COUNCIL

(advisers and officers appointed/dismissed by the King)

CHURCH

(bishops chosen by the King)

Local Government

in the County Community
1 Lord Lieutenant in each county, chosen by the King and Privy Council from the nobility/ greater gentry
2 JPs in counties and boroughs chosen and supervised by King and Privy Council on advice of Lord Lieutenant
3 Sheriff – formal role in holding elections
4 Chief Constables, Constables, Churchwardens and overseers of the Poor

Common Law Courts

<u>Central</u> – Exchequer; King's Bench; and Common Pleas
<u>Regional</u> – County Assizes held by judges appointed by the King
Quarter Sessions; Petty Sessions – both held by local JPs

Prerogative Courts

<u>Central</u> – Chancery; Star Chamber and High Commission
<u>Regional</u> – Councils of the North and Welsh Marches

Parish clergy

Electorate – mainly gentry and merchants but including some yeomen and master craftsmen

Figure 3 The structure of government in England and Wales in the sixteenth and seventeenth centuries. Compare with Figure 2 to see how government and social structure were linked.

An effective Lord Lieutenant was a major influence in the county. He could expect a circle of supporters among the gentry and borough officers, not only because of his position but also because he provided a path to influence and possible advancement in central government. The same was true to a lesser extent of the Deputy-Lieutenants, who were chosen to represent different county families and interests. In counties with more than one influential family, this could lead to feuds and factions which interacted with national issues and central government in influencing the loyalties of the governing class.

The strength of county identity has been a matter for some debate.

◢ Source

The allegiance of the provincial gentry to the community of their native shire is one of the basic facts of English history in the seventeenth and eighteenth centuries. Though the sense of national identity had been increasing since the early Tudors, so too had the sense of county identity... There were many factors in the development of regional loyalty: the growth of county administration, the development of county institutions, the expanding wealth of the local gentry, their increasing tendency to intermarriage, their growing interest in local history and legal custom, the rise of the county towns as social, cultural and administrative centres, [all]... entered into the rise of what Napier once called the 'county commonwealths' of England.

A. Everitt **The Local Community and the Great Rebellion** (1969)

Everitt's view has been challenged and modified by other local studies, which have shown it to apply much more in some counties than in others. (Many of these have been summarised in R. C. Richardson, *The Debate on the English Revolution Revisited*, 2nd edition, 1988.) Nevertheless, some sense of county identity existed in most areas, and could influence, or even distort, the impact of national issues and events across the different localities. This showed most clearly at times of crisis. But local loyalties always had the potential to cause problems, and required sensitive handling. The county gentry and merchants controlled, and expected to control, society in their own area. For this they needed the support of the King and the apparatus of law and government to guard against upheaval from below. At the same time, they resented excessive interference from the centre, and were aware that the monarch depended on their cooperation to enforce royal power in the regions. The relationship was therefore one of mutual dependence, with efficient government resting on a partnership between the king and the county community, and requiring mutual respect for royal authority and community rights.

While the Church, Privy Council and Prerogative Courts represented royal power, the functions of Parliament and the Common Law Courts were more complex. Both were controlled by the monarch, who called and dissolved parliament when he chose and who appointed judges at his pleasure. The functions of parliament were to advise the king, to grant taxation and to formalise royal decisions into legal statutes, the highest form of law. Both parliament and the law therefore existed to serve the king and to enhance royal power, but they also provided some restraints on his authority and freedom of action.

Parliament represented the county communities described above, being elected by the gentry and merchants with some of the better-off 'middling sort' of yeomanry and master craftsmen. Most MPs were amateurs, called occasionally to represent the views of their friends and neighbours and to assist the king in legalising and financing his decisions. They could, at times, carry out the first of these functions by refusing to carry out the second. In addition, it was assumed that the king should govern within the law, and that law at its highest was made in and with parliament. Just as efficient administration depended on a partnership of the monarchy and governing class, its legal and financial framework required that partnership to work in parliament. When Charles became king in 1625, the partnership, and the system that depended on it, was already showing signs of strain.

The sources of tension

The Tudor legacy

The inheritance Charles took up in 1625 was not easy. The century before his accession had been a period of rising population and price inflation, which had caused difficulties for both crown and people.

Social tensions

Rising food prices caused serious poverty for some, but stimulated agricultural production and the enclosure of land. Where this involved bringing new land under cultivation, it could be widely beneficial. But the land had often been utilised as wastes and commons, so that its enclosure robbed the poorer classes of valuable grazing rights or the right to collect food and fuel. More seriously, the development of the wool and cloth trades led to land being turned over to sheep, with a consequent loss of the jobs involved in arable farming. Unemployment and under-employment created a problem of vagabonds and 'sturdy beggars' which the government could not ignore. A series of Poor Laws, culminating in the Great Poor Law of 1601, helped to blunt the edge of popular unrest, but periodic shortages, land hunger and sporadic rioting continued until after the civil wars.

Financial problems

More seriously for the king, rising prices also helped to undermine royal finances. While Henry VIII inherited a full treasury, his entry into foreign wars had exhausted it by the time of the Reformation. The Dissolution of the Monasteries in 1536–9 provided an important new source of land and revenue, but some had to be passed on as gifts to the nobility and gentry in order to encourage their support, and more was sold to finance Henry's further military adventures in the 1640s. In addition, his debasement of the coinage in 1645, intended to raise funds, gave a further twist to the spiral of inflation.

By the reign of Elizabeth, financial problems were becoming significant. Short-term measures – such as the sale of crown lands – built up difficulties for her successors. For political reasons she failed to update tax assessments in line with inflated prices, although she did infuriate MPs and public alike by increasing sales of monopoly licences which removed competition, drove up prices and led to poor-quality goods. Most serious of all, however, was the long war against Spain that followed the Armada of 1588, which destroyed the effectiveness of Elizabeth's financial strategies. Whatever policies James adopted, there was no doubt that he would find himself financially dependent upon parliamentary taxes.

Religious divisions

Unfortunately, the financial problems of the period were accompanied by religious divisions. The Reformation created religious quarrels across Europe, and religious wars were fought within and between states. While England escaped the worst ravages of war, it suffered a period of religious instability after Henry VIII seized control of the Church by the Act of Supremacy in 1534. While Henry was motivated by personal and political considerations, his challenge to the authority of Rome forced him to ally with Protestant scholars and appoint them to positions of influence in the Church. Educated as a Protestant, the young Edward VI (1547–53) carried out a religious reformation. This was bloodily reversed by Mary (1553–8), whose burning of 300 Protestants and alliance with Spain were both deeply unpopular.

In the interests of stability, Elizabeth sought to establish a compromise in the Elizabethan settlement of 1558–9. The Anglican Church was undeniably Protestant in doctrine, rejecting the idea of **transubstantiation** as well as the authority of the Pope. It also rejected claims that the way to heaven lay through the Church and obedience to its rules, emphasising the Protestant belief in **justification by faith alone**.

KEY TERMS

Transubstantiation was the doctrine held by the Roman Catholic Church which claimed that the bread and wine used in the Mass (communion service) was miraculously transformed into the actual body and blood of Christ through the presence of God in the ceremony. This was one of the ideas rejected by Martin Luther and other Protestant leaders as foolish superstition.

Justification by faith alone – Protestants argued that salvation could only be achieved by faith, and as a free gift from God. Human beings could not earn salvation by what they did – only God could grant it, and this depended on the individual's direct relationship with God, not on the intervention or influence of the Church.

However, familiar and traditional ceremonies – such as the use of the cross in baptism and the ring in marriage, and the wearing of special clothes such as the surplice by priests – were maintained. These rules were laid out in the 1559 Prayer Book, along with formal prayers and catechisms which were to be used in certain services. In addition, the Church was to be organised and run by a hierarchy of priests, headed by bishops who were appointed by the Queen.

Like most compromises, it left dissatisfied minorities who sought further change. Small groups of Catholics were encouraged to plot against Elizabeth by Spain, leading to an expensive war from 1588 to 1604, and feeding the anti-Catholic paranoia of the other extreme Protestant minority known as **Puritans**.

KEY TERM

Puritan refers to those who wanted to purify the Anglican Church by getting rid of all traces of Catholic rituals and beliefs. Many of them had been particularly influenced by the ideas of John Calvin, a Protestant reformer who had founded a Church in the Swiss city of Geneva. Calvin's Church was famed for its simple services, emphasis on preaching and Bible study, and for the strict discipline exercised by the Minister and lay elders. The basis of his ideas was the doctrine of **'predestination'** – that God has chosen and predestined some people to be saved by their faith in him, while others are damned and sent to hell. This was a further development of the doctrine of 'justification by faith alone'. The outward sign of faith was membership of a Calvinist congregation, and acceptance of its strict rules, but Calvin's ideas also gave great power and independence to the individual, and encouraged private study and individual thinking. For this reason, such ideas did not appeal to monarchs like Elizabeth or James I, even though a form of Calvinism (known as Presbyterianism) had been adopted in the national Church of his native Scotland. Most English Protestants accepted many of Calvin's ideas; the Puritans simply wanted to take reform further.

The work of James I

James therefore inherited problems in three areas – religion, finance, and the difficulty of ruling three culturally distinct kingdoms – each of which caused tension between the king and the governing elite in parliament (see Figure 4 overleaf).

How might these results of the sixteenth-century Reformation and inflation interact to create difficulties for later monarchs? (If you want to find out more about any of these developments, see the 'further reading' section at the end of the book.)

Religious problems

Puritan reformers in the Church had considerable support among MPs, and had attempted reform through parliament. In response, Elizabeth forbade parliament to discuss the issue unless it was at her command, raising questions about parliamentary freedom. Frustrated by the queen, puritan ministers had attempted reform from within the Church itself, but had been crushed by the bishops under the leadership of Archbishop Whitgift. In 1603 they had high hopes of the Scottish James I, but James rejected their demands and enforced the existing rules.

In 1611, however, James appointed the moderate George Abbot as Archbishop, and a practical compromise developed, in which the more

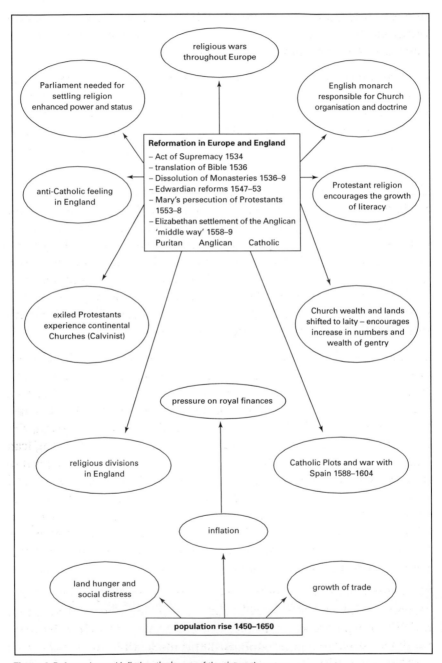

Figure 4 Reformation and inflation: the legacy of the sixteenth century

offensive rules and ceremonies to which the puritans objected were only occasionally enforced. As long as the bishops' authority was accepted, James and Abbot did not exercise it excessively.

By the end of James's reign, the Church encompassed three broad strands of opinion – Puritans, moderate Anglicans who accepted the Elizabethan compromise, and a traditionalist group known as Arminians, who sought to move the Church closer to its catholic origins. However, by his flexibility and carefully promoting ministers representing all opinions, James secured a large measure of peace in the Church.

The problem of multiple kingdoms
Similarly, after early clashes with the English parliament over his desire for a union of the English and Scottish crowns, James showed tact and diplomacy in the management of his three separate kingdoms. Scotland, Ireland and England/Wales had quite distinct political, religious and cultural traditions. While it was natural for the monarch to emphasise their common links, and to try to bring about greater uniformity of government within them, this would inevitably create resentment among those whose traditions were being weakened.

The most significant difficulty lay in religion, where regional variations were complicated by the rivalry between Protestant and Catholic faiths. In Scotland, a protestant reformation had created a Presbyterian Church, based on the Calvinist model (see key term, page 17), but had left a significant Catholic minority in the highlands. In England, the Elizabethan settlement had created a compromise: the Anglican Church, with a small Catholic minority and a much larger, puritan minority who wanted further Calvinist reform. In Ireland the catholic majority were feared and distrusted by their English rulers, who imposed an Anglican ruling Church and encouraged Protestants of all shades to settle on catholic land. James's own plantation policy increased this settlement with English Puritans and Scottish Presbyterians as well as the Anglican ruling class.

The complexity of the problem is clear, and it was only logical that a monarch would wish to establish uniform arrangements throughout the three kingdoms. The existence of a Presbyterian church in Scotland inevitably strengthened English puritan hopes, while the existence of catholic minorities increased their anti-Catholic fears. The Anglican

Church, with its powerful bishops, was the most compatible with royal authority. It was this model that James favoured and sought to extend. By 1621 he was able to persuade the Scots to restore bishops in an advisory role, but stopped short of establishing a Prayer Book in Scotland because of the depth of opposition to it. Throughout his reign he continued to be sensitive to Scottish opinion – in this as well as other areas – and to proceed towards greater uniformity with care and tact.

Financial problems

James's greatest weakness lay in his handling of finance, where his personal extravagance irritated parliament and his attempts to raise extra money led to open conflict. In 1606, in a test case involving the merchant Bates, the courts supported the king in imposing a new customs duty on currants. Then in 1608 a new Book of Rates imposed new or increased duties on all kinds of goods. These 'impositions' were bitterly opposed in parliament in 1610. An attempt to reform royal finances in a Great Contract with parliament failed, because of doubts on both sides. James continued to supplement his income by the sale of titles and monopolies, and to allow royal favourites such as the Duke of Buckingham to benefit from both. Efforts by Lionel Cranfield to balance the royal budget and reform its financial base in 1621–2 were thwarted by a combination of parliamentary hostility and the power of Buckingham. Parliament revived the medieval procedure of impeachment as a means of attacking royal advisers. In 1624 James was forced to accept an Act against Monopolies. By then, however, he was an ageing king who increasingly allowed the Duke of Buckingham, and his heir, Prince Charles, to conduct affairs.

Conclusion

There has been considerable debate regarding James I, and his responsibility for growing tensions between king and parliament in this period. There is little doubt that his personal habits, theoretical claims to a divine right of kings, and financial extravagance irritated many of the ruling class in parliament. But he handled many problems with skill and tact, and his decisions in practice were often effective. Certainly, he failed to solve the problems that he had inherited, but when he died in 1625 it is clear the monarchy was not on the brink of crisis.

The problems of religious divisions, in Britain and Europe, of multiple kingdoms and of financial and administrative weaknesses, were serious, but separate. James was able to deal with them as separate items, and to make some progress on that basis. As long as that was the case, it can be argued that the situation would remain manageable.

The impact of Charles I, 1625–42

Charles and Parliament, 1625–9

In 1624 Charles visited Spain to complete arrangements for a proposed marriage to the Spanish Infanta (princess). However, he was humiliated by the Spaniards, and pressed for war with Spain. Parliament supported the war, but finding it badly conducted, they showed their anger by granting only three subsidies in 1625, and refusing to vote the new King ***tunnage and poundage*** for life as was customary.

The war was placed in the hands of the DUKE OF BUCKINGHAM, who had negotiated a marriage for Charles with Henrietta Maria, sister of the King of France. Unfortunately, his incompetence led to further failures and to war with France. By 1626 parliament was threatening to impeach him and Charles dissolved parliament. This prevented a resolution of the dispute over tunnage and poundage, but Charles continued to collect the duties regardless. He also raised more money through a ***forced loan***, imprisoning those who refused to pay. In 1627 the judges upheld his right to do this in the Five Knights' Case.

KEY TERMS

Tunnage and poundage was the name given to customs duties, which formed an increasingly important part of royal revenues. It was normal for the first parliament of a reign to grant the right to levy these duties to the monarch for life. James, however, had increased the rate of duty and imposed duties on an increased range of goods, resulting in a quarrel with parliament in 1608–10. The issue had become entangled with plans for financial reform in the Great Contract of 1610, and had never been properly resolved, with the result that parliament withheld the grant for life from Charles and allowed him the revenues for one year only, pending clarification of the extent of his rights.

A **forced loan** involved exactly what it says – the king demanded that his subjects 'lend' him sums of money to offset government expenses. There was little doubt that the loans would be unlikely to be repaid, but the strategy had been used before and was considered acceptable in times of emergency. The problem with Charles's use of the idea was that the 'emergency' was partly of his own making, and that he was prepared to carry out his threats and punish those who refused.

Profile
DUKE OF BUCKINGHAM
1592–1628

George Villiers – the son of Sir George Villiers of Brooksby, Leicestershire – was educated at Billesdon School. This indicates his status as minor gentry, but his charm and good looks caught the attention of James I and opened the way to advancement in the King's Household. His advancement was rapid – Viscount Villiers in 1616, Earl of Buckingham in 1617, Marquis in 1618 and Duke of Buckingham in 1623. This, and the dubious nature of his influence, aroused resentment among the more established nobility, but his influence on James's policies was limited. He won the devotion of Charles during the disastrous visit to Madrid in 1623, and thereafter his political influence and significance increased. While he was quite capable of controlling and manipulating the factionalism of Court politics, as a statesman he lacked vision and purpose. His wars against Spain and France from 1624–7 were pointless and badly managed. When Buckingham was assassinated at Portsmouth in 1628, by an ex-army officer named John Felton, Charles was one of the few who grieved.

When it reassembled in 1628, parliament presented the Petition of Right. This demanded that the king should agree not to take forced loans, to imprison anyone without due cause shown, to billet soldiers with civilians, or to subject civilians to martial law. MPs also renewed their attacks on Buckingham, whose expedition to La Rochelle to help French Protestants in 1627 had ended in costly failure. To protect his favourite, Charles prorogued (suspended) parliament.

In August 1628 Buckingham was assassinated but this did not solve the underlying problems. Charles was angry about parliament's criticism, while MPs feared the king's arbitrary actions. Further clashes in 1629 led him to prorogue parliament once more, but when his message reached the Commons, angry MPs held the Speaker in his chair to prevent their dismissal while they passed three resolutions. These were:

◢ That anyone who encouraged or promoted Catholic or **Arminian** ideas in religion, or

◢ anyone who advised or encouraged the collection of tunnage and poundage without parliamentary consent, or

◢ anyone who voluntarily paid tunnage and poundage in those circumstances would be considered to be guilty of treason.

This act of defiance convinced Charles that he would govern more effectively without a parliament unless its role could be redefined. He dissolved parliament and arrested those responsible for the outrage.

KEY TERM

'**Arminian**' is derived from the Dutch theologian, Jacob Arminius, who had scandalised Calvinist Protestants by denying the doctrine that God predestined all people to be either saved or damned, arguing instead that humans had been given free will to either accept or reject the gift of salvation. This implied some return to the Catholic idea that salvation could be earned through the Church. Arminius's views were condemned at the Synod of Dort in 1618, but were taken up and adapted by a group of English scholars, notably Richard Montague and William Laud. The English Arminians adapted the original argument to emphasise the Church's authority and the importance of ceremonies and sacraments rather than preaching and bible-study – ideas which challenged Puritan thinking.

Religious problems, 1629–37

The Three Resolutions expressed parliamentary resentment of Charles's support for Arminian reformers in the Church. However, Charles was determined to press ahead with his plans. In 1628 he appointed William Laud as Bishop of London, and in 1633 Laud became Archbishop of Canterbury. He immediately began a programme of reform, and issued new instructions to the clergy that:

1 communion tables were to be removed to the east end of churches and railed off from the laity;

2 preaching was discouraged in favour of set prayers and catechisms;

3 only the nobility could maintain a private chaplain;

4 lecturers, who were paid to preach sermons, would be forced to carry out other services;

5 all rules and canons would be vigorously enforced through bishops' visitations and in the Church Courts.

The compromise built up by James was destroyed. Puritans lost lecture-ships, and faced having to leave the Church, or conform. Roman Catholics seemed to be better treated: a Roman Catholic group was developing around the queen, a Catholic. Lord Weston was made Lord Treasurer, and in 1637 Charles welcomed an envoy from the Pope at Court.

Bishops had great influence in government and Laud dominated the Privy Council. Puritans who protested were brutally treated: in 1637 Burton, Bastwick and Prynne, who published criticism of Laud and the Queen, had their ears clipped. Prynne was also branded. These types of punishments were not normally inflicted on educated people, and contemporaries were shocked. Nevertheless, there seemed to be little that they could do to halt the king's plans.

Personal government, 1629–37

After the crisis of 1628–9, Charles wanted government, State and Church reform. Sir Thomas Wentworth was made President of the Council of the North, and a member of the Privy Council in 1629. In 1632 he became Lord Deputy of Ireland, and Lord Strafford. The common purpose shared by Charles, Laud and Strafford was to create efficient government through close central supervision – a policy known as 'Thorough'.

This was accompanied by new financial policies to increase govern-ment resources, reduce debts and secure financial independence from parliament. Monopolies were sold again and forest laws and feudal pay-ments were revived. Most successful was the introduction of ship-money – an ancient, occasional tax levied on ports, which was now extended to the whole country and levied annually. In 1637 when John Hampden contested the tax in court, the judges found for the king.

By 1637, Charles had apparently established a personal government free of parliamentary or financial constraints. What changed the situa-tion was the ill-fated attempt in 1637 to impose a revised English Prayer Book on the presbyterian Church of Scotland.

The Scottish Rebellion, 1637–40

Charles was determined to create uniformity in the three kingdoms that he ruled as separate units. James had made some progress in this area, but he had proceeded slowly and tactfully. Charles, however, lacked such caution. Both the strength of his convictions and his autocratic nature drove him forward.

In 1637 the use of the Prayer Book in St Giles Cathedral in Edinburgh sparked off a riot which turned to a widespread rebellion (see Figure 5). In 1638 a National Covenant (agreement) was set up to defend the Presbyterian system. The Covenanters raised an army which Charles couldn't defeat, and in 1639 he was forced to sign the Treaty of Berwick, which allowed the Scots to abolish the Bishops and the Prayer Book.

Charles could not accept this, and recalled Strafford from Ireland. He advised the king to call a parliament, hoping to exploit traditional anti-Scottish feeling, but MPs insisted on addressing grievances before supplies. Charles dissolved this Short Parliament and renewed the war, but was again defeated. With a Scottish army in England he was forced to accept the Treaty of Ripon, and to call a parliament. On 3 November 1640 the parliament that was to be known as the Long Parliament assembled at Westminster.

Figure 5 A woodcut showing what supposedly happened when the local priest tried to use the new Prayer Book in St Giles Cathedral, Edinburgh, in 1637

The redress of grievances, 1640–41

The calling of the Long Parliament brought the crisis to a head, but war was not the inevitable outcome. In 1640 MPs expected compromise, and even Charles accepted that he would have to make concessions. In February 1641 he reluctantly accepted the Triennial Act which guaranteed parliament meeting at least once every three years. Laud was impeached. To remove Strafford, the opposition introduced a Bill of Attainder which, if passed by parliament, would simply declare him legally guilty. This required the King's consent, which he refused.

Pym, the main leader of the opposition group in the House of Commons, raised the political heat by revealing a plot among the King's more extreme supporters to dissolve parliament by force (the First Army Plot). Popular demonstrations outside the House of Lords and then Whitehall intimidated both the Lords and the King into sanctioning Strafford's death. In May 1641 Strafford was executed. In July, ship-money and other non-parliamentary taxation was declared to be illegal, and the Prerogative Courts were abolished.

However, by the early summer of 1641, there were signs of disagreement among MPs. In May the Commons had passed a bill to exclude bishops from the House of Lords, but in June this was rejected by the Upper House. This was followed by the Root and Branch Bill which abolished bishops in the Church but it had to be laid aside as it clearly would not pass the Commons. The Ten Propositions put to the king before he visited Scotland sought to give parliament influence over his choice of advisers, and many MPs felt that this was going too far in changing the balance of the constitution. Led by Edward Hyde, a group of moderate royalists were emerging in support of the king.

The summer of 1641 therefore saw a political stalemate, but in October/November of that year the outbreak of a Catholic rebellion in Ireland and rumours that thousands of Protestants were being massacred raised a new problem. It was clear that an army would be needed, and parliament was willing to vote supplies. The problem for the opposition was that, while they desired to rescue Ireland, they dared not place an army in the hands of a king whom they distrusted. They therefore decided to attach a condition to the Militia Bill which would enable a parliament to control the choice of army commander.

The drift to war, 1641–2

To gain support for this, Pym introduced a Grand Remonstrance in the House of Commons in November, which was published in December. It set out the opposition case, but infuriated the more cautious members and provoked the king into action. On 4 January he entered the House of Commons with 300 armed men in order to arrest five members (in addition to Lord Kimbolton, later the Earl of Manchester) whom he considered to be the opposition leaders, only to find that they had been warned in time to escape.

The action convinced MPs that the king was willing to use force. Amid popular demonstrations the king left London, and both sides began to make defensive preparations for possible war. In June parliament initiated a final attempt at negotiation in the Nineteen Propositions, but their demands were too extreme to make a peaceful outcome realistic. In the same month, both parties sent out orders to raise troops. In August the King made the final, decisive move when he raised his standard at Nottingham and called for volunteers.

The fall and rise of the monarchy, 1642–60

War and defeat, 1642–6

At the beginning of the war the advantage lay with the King, and his best chances of victory came in 1642–3. However, strategic errors and the determined resistance of parliamentary outposts prevented him from grasping the opportunity. In 1643 John Pym succeeded in negotiating a parliamentary alliance with the Scots, and parliament's long-term advantages in controlling the south-east, the major ports and the navy began to take effect. In 1644 the parliamentary victory at Marston Moor secured the north for parliament, although the advantage was squandered by political divisions and the reluctance of parliament's aristocratic commanders to take the war to the king.

Early in 1645 the removal of these generals and the creation of a single, mobile army – a New Model Army – under the command of Sir Thomas Fairfax and Oliver Cromwell initiated the final phase of the war. In June the king's error in challenging this army when outnumbered led to his defeat at Naseby and to the surrender of his headquarters at Oxford in 1646. By that time, he had already surrendered to the Scots, who promptly handed him over to parliamentary forces and to genteel imprisonment at Holdenby House in Northamptonshire.

The failure of negotiations, 1646–9

Negotiations for settlement were initiated by parliament. However, Charles had no intention of surrendering his powers or accepting puritan reform of the Church. Early in 1647 he appeared to have the opportunity he required when divisions appeared among parliament's supporters. Conservatives in parliament, concerned by the emergence of radical religious groups in and around the New Model Army, attempted to disband the army without settling arrears of pay. This led to army mutinies and the emergence of the army as a third political force.

For Charles this appeared to provide the chance to exploit divisions among his opponents, and when the army leaders presented him with their own (generous) terms for settlement, he delayed his answer to buy time. In the meanwhile he negotiated with the Scots, whose rigid Presbyterianism was even more deeply offended by radical ideas than were their allies in the English parliament. Convinced that he had no moral obligation to deal honestly with rebels, in December 1647 Charles concluded a secret engagement by which the Scots were to invade England and restore him to his throne in return for the temporary establishment of Presbyterianism in England.

By this action, Charles initiated a second civil war, and signed his own death warrant. The military threat from Scotland and various scattered royalist risings were dealt with by the New Model Army. By September 1648 the war was over. It had, however, transformed the Army's attitude to the king. He was declared a 'man of blood' who had abused his powers, made war on his people and deserved to be brought to account for all the deaths and destruction resulting from it. He had rejected God's verdict on his actions, made clear by his defeat in 1646, and shown himself to be untrustworthy. The Army demanded that he should be brought to trial and punished for his crimes.

The conservative majority in parliament rejected this call, and tried to renew negotiations with Charles but he made few meaningful concessions. Convinced not only of his divine right and status but also that no settlement could be made without him, he threatened his opponents that 'without me you will fall'. The Army's response was to purge parliament of those who wished to continue negotiating, allowing the minority remnant, or 'Rump', of MPs to set up a High Court, bring the King to trial and find him guilty of treason. On 30 January 1649 Charles was beheaded outside his palace of Whitehall.

Republic and restoration

Two months later the monarchy and House of Lords were formally abolished and England declared a republic. Yet this republic lasted little more than 11 years. In May 1660 Charles's eldest son, Charles II, returned as king with most of his father's powers intact. The explanation for this astonishing reversal lies partly in errors, divisions and weaknesses among republican supporters, but two points are very clear. The first is that the republic was the work of a minority, who would find it hard to win the support of the nation. The second is that, in the manner of his death, Charles served the cause of monarchy far better than he ever had in his life.

Taking his stand upon the illegality of his trial, he was able to present the monarchy as the symbol of law, justice and the subject's rights. Dying with great dignity and courage, he was able to inspire a potent myth of the martyr king, which was then built upon by royalist propaganda. When royalist writers published the supposed last thoughts and writings of Charles the Martyr in the book *Eikon Basilike*, it sold in vast quantities and went through reprint after reprint. The fact was that monarchy was deeply rooted in popular affections, intertwined with the law, and deemed to be the guarantee of order and stability.

This did not mean that no alternative could succeed, but that the task would be a difficult one, made more difficult by the circumstances of Charles's death. It could therefore be said that he made two contributions to the development of the English monarchy: through his errors and misjudgements in bringing about its collapse, and through the manner of his death in helping to bring about its return. What remains debatable is the significance of both in the long term.

1 Effective note-making

Note-making is often undervalued by students, who complain that it is time-consuming and boring. The first complaint is accurate, at least until you learn to do it well; the second is not! If making notes is boring, it usually means that you are copying, not thinking.

Good notes should be:
- set out in clear sections, with clear headings and subheadings
- well-spaced and abbreviated
- made up of clearly stated points with some examples and useful phrases and quotes attached beneath the main point.

It takes time to practise but is of enormous help. First, you will have to think about what you are reading in order to decide what should go in each section and you will only be able to do it if you understand the material. Therefore you will be learning as you go. Writing the notes will also help you to remember what you learn. Secondly, by including good phrases and quotes, you will be building up a vocabulary for essay-writing. Thirdly, these notes are easy to revise from.

As a starting-point, you could use the sections on the 'Tudor legacy' and the work of James I. This is background information and you do not need great detail, but it will help you to understand the reign of Charles I if you have already defined the issues with which Charles was dealing. It will also help you later to assess how well, or how badly, Charles handled them. The section covers problems in four areas:
- religion and the Church
- finance
- King and parliament
- multiple kingdoms.

Use these as main headings, set out on separate pieces of paper. For each one, you can summarise the problem up to 1625, using the subheading 'Origins'. You can then read the narrative outline of Charles's reign and make notes about the development and effects of each problem. Set these out as subheadings in each section, and keep your notes for each one brief and specific. Include names and dates where useful. Use abbreviations where you can. If you get used to doing this, it will also help you to keep up when taking notes as someone is speaking – for example, in a lecture or discussion.

TASKS

This method, known as taking linear notes, is the most effective way of recording information. There are other kinds of notes, involving diagrams of various kinds, such as the timeline (see page 7 for example), flow charts and spider diagrams such as the diagrams used in Figures 2 and 3. These can sometimes summarise information, but are particularly useful for outlining a process and establishing links between different factors. You may find it useful to construct some diagrams of your own, using the information in your linear notes. As you become more experienced, you will develop your own applications of these techniques and learn which ones are most effective for you.

By the time you have completed these notes, you should be able to describe briefly the problems that Charles faced when he came to the throne in 1625, and how he dealt with them. You will then find it much easier to tackle the tasks set out below.

2a Using the outline of events before and during the reign of Charles I and the chronological table (pages 7–8), construct a timeline to show the causes of the Civil War. You should restrict yourself to one sheet of A4 paper. This will probably mean that you will have to select some events from a greater number and therefore make judgements about which events were most important. You can then compare this with the choices that others make, and discuss the reasons for your judgements.

  b When you have finalised your timeline, use different colours to code the events relating to religion, finance, King and parliament, and multiple kingdoms. You will find that some events relate to more than one problem – and this will help you to consider how different problems and factors combined and interacted to bring about Civil War.

3 Finally, using all the ideas that you have developed through tasks 1 and 2, you should write out a brief explanation of why civil war broke out in England in 1642. The explanation should cover five factors:
- religion and the church
- financial problems of the Crown
- tensions between king and parliament

◢ the effects of multiple kingdoms

◢ and the character and actions of Charles I.

4 The exercises above will help you to understand how the crisis in government developed, but there may be points which require deeper analysis and explanation. One way of approaching this is through an examination of sources relating to a particular issue. If we consider the question, *Why did civil war break out in 1642?*, the approach in tasks 1–3 will encourage us to look at a range of factors operating over a period of time, whereas the source exercise below leads us to consider what motives and factors influenced men to take up arms in the final stages. The two approaches are complementary, arising from slightly different interpretations of the question, and offering different insights into the issues involved.

5 Taking up arms, 1642

    a Read sources A–F, and answer these questions:

      i What evidence suggests that people took up arms on the basis of:

        – religious views?

        – political beliefs?

        – class loyalties?

      ii What evidence suggests that they were influenced by local issues and interests?

      iii In what ways were these motives conflicting?

    b Using all the evidence that you have collected, explain how and why men took up arms in 1642.

◢ Source A

Before the flame of the war broke out in the top of the chimneys, the smoke ascended in every country. The king had sent forth commissions of array, and the parliament had given out commissions for their militia. Between these, in many places, there were fierce contests and disputes... for in the progress every county had the civil war (more or less) within itself. Some counties were in the beginning so wholly for the parliament that the king's interest appeared not in them; some so wholly for the king that the godly (for those generally were the parliament's friends) were forced to forsake their habitations and seek other shelters.

> From Lucy Hutchinson, **Memoirs of the Life of Colonel Hutchinson** (1660)

◢ Source B

King Charles had a complaint against him for his wenching. Henry was in Hyde Park one time when his Majesty espied him and said, 'Let that ugly rascal be gone out of the park, that whoremaster.' Henry went away patiently, but it lay stored up in his heart. That sarcasm raised the whole county of Berkshire against the King.

> From John Aubrey, **Brief Lives** (1691) – referring to a Berkshire gentleman, Henry Marton

◢ Source C

... The greatest family was the Earl of Newcastle's [commander of the king's northern armies]. He had indeed, through his great estate, his liberal hospitality and constant residence in his country, so endeared [the gentry and their dependents] to him that no man was a greater prince in all that northern quarter... Most of the gentry... were disaffected to the parliament. Most of the middle sort – the able substantial freeholders and the other commons who had not their dependence upon the malignant nobility and gentry – adhered to the parliament... Mr Henry Ireton... was the chief promoter of the parliament's interest in the county. But finding it generally disaffected, all he could do when the king approached it was to gather a troop of those godly people which the cavaliers drove out, and with them to go into the army of my Lord of Essex.

> From Lucy Hutchinson, **Memoirs** – referring to the county of Nottinghamshire

◢ Source D

In Leicestershire leadership was divided between Henry Hastings [Royalist] and the Puritan Lord Grey of Groby. This division was much more than a rivalry between Puritan and Cavalier, however. The division between the two families went back to personal feuds and rivalry for control of the county since the mid-sixteenth century. According to Clarendon the whole county was divided between the Greys and the Hastingses. Local circumstances forced the gentry to take sides.

> From A. Everitt, **The Local Community and the Great Rebellion**

◢ Source E

Far more decisive than any socio-economic correlations is that with religion. In Yorkshire over one-third of the Royalist gentry were Catholics and over a half of the Parliamentarians were Puritans. To put it another way, of those who took sides, 90 per cent of all Catholics became Royalists, and 72 per cent of all Puritans became Parliamentarians. All the parliamentary leaders in Yorkshire had a previous record of strong Puritan sympathies. There is reason to think those who had opposed the Crown on purely constitutional and political grounds in the 1620s and 1630s tended to swing back to the king with Sir Edward Hyde in 1642, while those who had also opposed the Crown on religious grounds were far more likely to stick to Pym and fight for the Parliamentary cause.

From Lawrence Stone, **The Causes of the English Revolution, 1529–1642** (Routledge, 1972)

◢ Source F

They who were most inclined to the parliament, whereof the Lord Fairfax and his son were the chief... [preferred] to look on [rather] than engage themselves in the war. [And the royalist commander, Sir Thomas Glemham] was not... able to infuse fire enough into the phlegmatic constitutions of [his] people. Who did rather wish to be spectators of the war than parties in it, and believed, if they did not provoke the other party, they might all live quietly together; until Sir John Hotham, by his excursions and depredations out of Hull, and their seditious neighbours, by their insurrections, awakened them out of that pleasant dream.

From Clarendon, **The History of the Great Rebellion** – written in exile between 1646 and 1660. This passage describes neutralism among the county gentry of Yorkshire.

PART TWO

CHAPTER ONE

CHARLES I: MAN AND KING

Objectives

⊿ To investigate the part played by Charles I in causing the political crisis of 1640

⊿ To assess the king's character and to determine how divisive an influence he was

The role of individuals in historical development is an area much debated by historians, but few would challenge the argument that Charles I played a significant part in causing the political crisis of 1640 and the war of 1642. As Conrad Russell puts it, in his book *The Causes of the Civil War*, there was 'a remarkably swift general recognition, during Charles's first year, that as a king he was not a success, and that judgement is one that has never been reversed'.

Part 1 has already shown how the king's attitudes and actions provoked opposition, and how his errors and misjudgements brought the crisis to a head and eventually to armed conflict. Nevertheless, the issue of Charles's importance as an individual and the significance of his personality remain a matter of debate.

The individual in history

In order to consider his individual importance we have to isolate actions that would not have been taken by other monarchs of the time, and show that these can be attributed to Charles's personality. It is not sufficient to demonstrate that he tried to enforce uniformity in the Church, to assert royal authority, or even that he was prepared to use force against those whom he regarded as rebels, for these patterns of belief and behaviour were common to most seventeenth-century monarchs, and to Charles's predecessors. What has to be shown by those who would attribute significance to Charles as an individual is that his beliefs and actions were in some way different to, or more extreme than, the norm, and that these differences played a significant part in causing the crisis of 1640 and its eventual outcomes.

Figure 6 A painting of Charles I by Van Dyck from 1635 showing the king of England from three different angles

This is not necessarily a straightforward task. Relatively little is known of Charles before his accession to the throne – a fact which may in itself be significant – and as a monarch, he was notoriously unwilling to expose his deeper feelings and beliefs. Evidence is therefore limited to his actions (which may well have been influenced by external pressures) and to the speeches, proclamations and correspondence that were produced during his reign, often for some public or political purpose. It is important, therefore, that sources from and about Charles as king are carefully evaluated and interpreted *in context*. With this qualification, they can suggest answers to two key questions:

1 Did Charles subscribe to particular political or religious beliefs that made him less able than other monarchs to deal successfully with the situation that he inherited in 1625?

2 Did Charles have a distinctive personality or temperament that might have a similar effect?

If the answer to either of these questions is affirmative, then it can be argued that Charles, *as an individual*, had a significant influence on the causes and outcome of the seventeenth-century crisis.

Politics and the Constitution

The powers of a king

The majority of Englishmen were agreed in 1625, that England enjoyed a mixed monarchy in which government was by king-in-parliament. The meaning of this phrase is demonstrated in the two sources below, which describe the King as having both 'ordinary' and 'absolute' power, and as carrying out some functions of government alone, others in and with parliament.

◢ Source 1

The king's power is double, ordinary and absolute... That of the ordinary is for the profit of particular subjects, for the execution of civil justice, and this is exercised by equity and justice in ordinary courts, and is known as common law, and these laws cannot be changed without parliament. The absolute power of the king is... that which is applied to the general benefit of the people, and this power is most properly named policy and government. This absolute power varies according to the wisdom of the king for the common good; and these being general... all things done within these rules are lawful.

The Judgement of Chief Baron Fleming in Bates's Case (1606)

◢ Source 2

The king distributes his authority and power in the fashion of five things: in the making of laws and ordinances; in the making of battle and peace with foreign nations; in providing of money for the maintenance of himself and defence against his enemies; in choosing and election of the chief officers and magistrates; and fifthly, in the administration of justice. The first and third are done by the prince [king] in parliament. The second and fourth by the prince [king] himself. The fifth is by the great assize [law courts].

Sir Thomas Smith, **De Republica Anglorum** (1583)

Charles's 'absolute' (prerogative) power allowed him to make decisions and to act, but it was widely recognised that the king should normally govern within the law. This relationship is outlined in source 3 by James I, whose high-sounding claims of Divine Right often irritated MPs, but who nevertheless respected their beliefs in practice.

◢ Source 3

Kings are justly called gods for that they exercise a manner or resemblance of divine power upon earth ... In the first original of kings, whereof some had their beginning by conquest and some by election of the people, their wills at that time served for law. Yet [when] kingdoms began to be settled in civility and policy, then did kings set down their minds by laws ... A king governing in a settled kingdom leaves to be a king and degenerates into a tyrant as soon as he leaves off to rule according to his laws ...

From a speech delivered to parliament by James I on 26 March 1610

Differences between monarch and parliament up to 1625 were largely a matter of emphasis; but there were two unsolved problem areas: the first involved the precise balance of royal prerogative and parliamentary rights where they differed over an issue; the second was what action could be taken by subjects if their monarch should, in James's words, 'leave to be a king' and act in an unjust or unlawful way. James offered no theoretical solution, but in practice he behaved with a measure of tact and respect for legal restraints.

The attitudes and beliefs of Charles I

In comparison to his father, Charles rarely explained or expressed his political beliefs as a coherent theory. But when he did, there is little to indicate that his ideas were particularly authoritarian. In 1642 his declarations and justification of his cause were firmly rooted in conventional ideas of law, and government by king-in-parliament. His response to the Newcastle Propositions of 1646, and to his trial in 1649, had changed little from his reply to the Nineteen Propositions of 1642, accusing parliament's supporters of behaving illegally and arbitrarily. While these sources must be treated with caution, since they were all framed for propaganda purposes, their main points were echoed in a private letter written to the Prince of Wales in 1649, on the eve of Charles's execution (source 4). Charles begins by emphasising the importance of the Church as a pillar of monarchy, closely followed by the law and parliaments.

◢ Source 4

The next main hinge on which your prosperity will depend and move, is that of civil justice, wherein the settled laws of these kingdoms, to which you are rightly heir, are the most excellent rules you can govern by ... Nor would I have you entertain any aversion or dislike of Parliaments, which, in their right constitution with freedom and honour, will never hinder or diminish your greatness, but will rather be an interchanging of love, loyalty and confidence, between a prince and his people.

Letter of Charles I, 29 January 1649, quoted in
C. W. Daniels and J. Morrill **Charles I** (CUP, 1994)

It seems unlikely that Charles would be expressing anything other than his genuine convictions in this situation, and on this evidence there is little in his political or constitutional ideas that contemporaries would have found offensive. Nor, since he was about to die for his refusal to compromise, is there any reason to believe that he had undergone some radical conversion in his ideas.

The real problem with Charles lay not in what he believed, but in how he interpreted those beliefs in practice. One clue to this lies in his reference to parliaments 'in their right constitution'. Charles did not oppose the idea of parliaments, nor deny the importance of parliamentary law, but he did reserve to himself the right to override both in pursuit of his duty as he saw it. This was incorporated in seventeenth-century constitutional thinking as the 'royal prerogative' – the 'absolute' power described in source 1. The problem was that Charles asserted his right to use this power both more extensively and more frequently than was politically wise or acceptable. When his actions created opposition, he responded with an anger that could easily appear vindictive.

The point is illustrated by the Forced Loan, and the Five Knights' Case (see timeline on page 7). When Charles dissolved parliament in 1626 to protect Buckingham, and thereby lost his subsidies, he felt totally justified in demanding the same amount in a forced loan. In his view the situation was forced upon him by the behaviour of MPs in overstepping their 'right constitution' and attacking his favourite, the Duke of Buckingham. Having a war to fight and fund, he saw:

◢ Source 5

no other possible and present course to be taken, nor this to be avoided, if we as a King shall maintain the cause and party of religion, preserve our own honour, defend our people, secure our kingdoms and support our allies, all which we are tied to do by that bond of sovereignty, which under God we bear over you.

Royal Proclamation, 7 October 1626

Charles was by no means the first monarch to levy such a loan, but when faced with resistance and refusal to pay, he ordered harsh punishments. The wealthy were to be imprisoned, the less wealthy to be conscripted into the army or have soldiers billeted on them. When his actions were challenged in the Five Knights' Case, Charles produced a string of precedents to justify such 'prerogative' imprisonment and insisted that the judges enter them as binding for the future. In doing what he believed to be necessary for governing, he was laying a practical foundation for tyranny.

The Proclamation is significant and revealing in several ways. First, it defines Charles's idea of the aims and purpose of government, setting out duties and objectives that he consistently worked for throughout his reign. The Personal Rule of 1629–40 was seen by some as an 11-year tyranny, but for Charles it was a period of reform, order and good government. Reforms in the Church, the establishment of sound royal finance through various fiscal devices, the use of the Prerogative Courts to administer speedy and impartial justice – these were laudable aims and practices in the eyes of the king who applied them. If they were seen differently by others it was because of their malice or foolishness, not because the measures were wrong in themselves. Nor, as the Proclamation of 1626 further reveals, was Charles unwilling to explain or justify his decisions. In the political turbulence of the 1620s, the years of personal rule and in the period of the Long Parliament, Charles publicly declared his aims and intentions and the reasons behind them. The difficulty lay in his assumption that these declarations must be accepted by his dutiful subjects, and his inability to understand why some were unable to do so. If he had no intention of using his powers unjustly, then there was no reason but malice for anyone to challenge them. What Charles suffered from was not authoritarian beliefs, but naive assumptions regarding the use of his powers and an authoritarian manner of applying them.

He also had a clear and simple answer to the question of how subjects should behave if the sovereign broke the law. This was explained in the sermons of Richard Sibthorpe which Charles had printed and published during the forced loan controversy.

◢ Source 6

Subjects are bound to obedience [declared Sibthorpe] by the double obligation of Justice and of Necessity... If a prince impose an immoderate, yea an unjust tax, yet the subject may not thereupon withdraw his obedience and duty. Nay, he is bound in conscience to submit, as under the scourge of sin ... Oh let us not then conceive to ourselves a Conscience grounded upon suspicious conjectures; concerning which, no man can ever set down certainties; and we are bound to believe the best concerning all men, much more concerning sovereigns' promises...

R. Sibthorpe, 'Apostolic Obedience', 1627 quoted in Daniels and Morrill, **Charles I**

In Charles's eyes, the role of subjects was obedience and it was unacceptable to even question the premises upon which a king made his decisions. A king must answer to his conscience, and this Charles genuinely did. If, therefore, he knew his intentions to be honourable, and declared them to be so, then no honest man could entertain valid doubts. The point was emphasised in 1640 when the French ambassador wrote that Charles was seeking a parliament which would confine itself to discussing the Scottish problem. His dismissal of the Short Parliament was not the result of a desire to do without parliament, but of impatience with a parliament that would not concentrate on the matter in hand. According to Conrad Russell he was 'crediting Charles with a temperamental, not a constitutional arbitrariness. He was not accused of intending to do without parliaments, but of forcing them to adopt his perspective and his point of view as a condition of doing business with him. Tunnel vision surely goes farther than constitutional theory towards explaining such a position.'

The character and personality of Charles I

What is implied by these arguments is that it was not Charles's beliefs that created difficulties but his personality. According to Charles Carlton, who has made a psychological study of the king, he developed an authoritarian personality to cover an underlying sense of inadequacy.

◢ Source 7

In psychological terms Charles's early years had produced an overdeveloped superego that bottled up his inner tensions. Charles tried to protect himself by seeking affection, currying favour, becoming withdrawn, displaying deference rare in an heir, and above all by submitting. Thus when he became king he expected similar behaviour, demanded a similar sacrifice, and insisted upon as great and painful a loyalty as he had been forced to yield. An authoritarian personality, Charles was incapable of conceding at a time when compromises were desperately demanded from the English monarchy. He was full of outward self-certainty (manifest in such doctrines as divine right) that only intense inner doubt can engender...

C. Carlton, in J. G. A. Pocock (ed.) **Three British Revolutions**
(Folger Shakespeare Library, 1981)

Whether or not it is possible to understand the psychology of the past, there is certainly much in Charles's life that can be explained by this lethal combination of private doubt and public authority.

Charles was the second son of James, and his youth was overshadowed by the presence and then death of his popular brother, Prince Henry. In contrast Charles was shy, a poor speaker and inclined to take refuge in formality. This was illustrated by the arrangements that he introduced at Court, replacing the chaotic and sometimes corrupt court of James with a dignified and studied formality. Access to the king's private apartments was denied to all but a few, and when entry was permitted, Charles insisted that the nobility were presented in strict order of rank. His lack of confidence was probably also responsible for the reliance on Buckingham which did so much to sour the early years of his reign. Although he never demonstrated such dependence on those who served him in later years, Buckingham's place was partly filled by the queen, Henrietta Maria. After a difficult start the marriage became a close and happy one, possibly because Buckingham's assassination created a gap in Charles's life which his queen was able to fill.

The influence of the Queen

Unfortunately her advice and influence was, like Buckingham's, politically damaging. Believing that Charles's problems arose because he was not sufficiently assertive, she constantly encouraged his authoritarianism when it was at its most dangerous. In January 1641 the Venetian ambassador wrote that 'she feels very strongly at seeing her husband... effectively despised by his own subjects. For this reason she never ceases to urge him to throw himself into desperate courses.' (A month later she attempted to borrow money from the Catholic Church to solve Charles's difficulties.) In February 1642 she crossed to Holland to raise money and troops. According to the Venetian ambassador, 'The Queen told me positively that to settle affairs it was necessary to unsettle them first, as she considered it impossible to re-establish her husband's authority in any other way.' A month later she was writing to Charles, urging him 'do not break your resolution, but follow it constantly and do not lose time', and reminding him that 'you have already learned to your cost that want of perseverance in your designs has ruined you'.

These events are likely to have influenced the description of Charles's character provided by Edward Hyde, Lord Clarendon, in his monumental *History of the Great Rebellion*. Although a royalist and naturally sympathetic to Charles, Clarendon did attempt to maintain some balance in his judgements, and his assessment may well be reasonably accurate as far as it goes.

◢ Source 8

... he will be found not only a prince of admirable virtue and piety, but of great parts of knowledge, wisdom and judgement; and that the most signal parts of his misfortunes proceeded chiefly from the modesty of his nature, which kept him from trusting himself enough, and made him believe that others discerned better, who were much inferior to him in those faculties; and so to depart often from his own reason, to follow the

opinions of more unskilful men, whose affections he believed to be unquestionable to his service...

G. Huehns (ed.) ***Clarendon: Selections*** *(Oxford University Press, 1978)*

Throughout the 1640s, advisers like Hyde who sought to guide Charles into compromises that would have left much of his power intact found themselves counteracted by the influence of the queen and others like her. In 1641 Charles was enormously damaged by the activities of Sir John Ashburnham and his fellow conspirators in the Army plots, but refused to disown them. What Clarendon does not say is that these more assertive counsels may well have appealed to Charles because they reflected his own resentment of opposition and his desire to act, as he saw it, firmly and with strength.

More seriously, this combination of uncertainty and authoritarianism in Charles's character may well explain the accusations of indecisiveness and deceit that have been levelled at him. Charles was not unintelligent, and was fully capable of seeing the value of Hyde's tactics. What he did not share was the moderate vision that lay behind such advice – hence there was a constant temptation to listen to more rash counsels that accorded more closely with his own underlying feelings. As a result, neither path was followed consistently, and the impression was created that Charles's word could not be trusted.

The mistrust that was therefore built up was the main obstacle in the way of the negotiated settlement that would have prevented the outbreak of Civil War. No incident illustrates this more clearly than the attempted arrest of the Five Members in January 1642, when Charles undid in a few hours the months of patient work that his supporters had devoted to building up a royalist party in parliament. Throughout the years that followed, those of the king's advisers who sought a negotiated peace, were constantly thwarted by military advisers like Prince Rupert, and by the more hot-headed royalists like Lord Digby, who encouraged the king to seek outright victory. More seriously, Charles's failure to commit himself fully to any one of these strategies led to internal rivalries, uncertain policies and fatal errors. In 1645, Digby's rivalry with Prince Rupert goaded him into encouraging Charles to fight the disastrous Battle of Naseby; his foolishness was matched by

Charles himself, who chose to ignore the advice of his military experts in favour of the arguments that he wanted to hear.

Religion and the Church

If Charles's constitutional views were broadly conventional, his ideas on religion and the Church posed greater problems. Again there are few sources to reveal his views on salvation or Biblical authority, but there is no reason to doubt that his faith was essentially Protestant. However, he was not a Calvinist and probably accepted Arminian arguments on salvation (see key term, page 23). English Arminians like William Laud adapted the doctrine to increase the role of the Church in guiding souls to salvation. This offended English puritans in two ways: it was uncomfortably close to the Catholic doctrine of salvation through good works (good works including attendance at church and obedience to the Catholic Church); secondly, it emphasised authority and public profession above individual study and belief.

Once again it was Charles's temperament and the means that he chose to apply his beliefs that created the most serious difficulties. These arose from three areas. The first was his emphasis on order and decency in the Church. Here again, Charles's personality – his reserve, his liking for formality and his almost obsessional concern with decent order – gave a distinctive character to his religious views and policies. The second was his emphasis on authority, in particular on clerical authority. The third, and probably the most dangerous politically, was his attitude towards Catholicism and the Church of Rome. In all of these areas Charles was supported and served by the Arminian minority in the Church, whom he favoured and promoted exclusively. In this he lacked the political sense of both James and Elizabeth, who had been careful to maintain a balance among the different parties in their distribution of patronage. Even worse, in all of these areas he was at odds with the hopes and fears of the majority of his subjects.

Order, decency and authority

The attempt by Charles and Laud to restore the condition of the Church to 'the beauty of holiness' was not unreasonable. There is plentiful evidence that churches were used for all kinds of activities, from conducting business to archery practice, and that churchyards were even more commonly abused. However, the kind of decency that they envisaged emphasised traditional ceremonies that were widely regarded as remnants of popery. They cut across the puritan emphasis on preaching and teaching; they represented and enhanced the status and authority of the clergy in general and the Bishops in particular. Laud argued the case in an open letter to Charles:

◢ Source 9

This I have observed farther, that no one thing hath made conscientious men more wavering in their own minds or more apt and easy to be drawn aside from the sincerity of religion professed by the Church of England, than the want of uniform and decent order in too many churches of the kingdom... It is true, the inward worship of the heart is the great service of God... but the external worship of God in his Church is the great witness to the world, that our heart stands right in that service... Now, no external action in the world can be uniform without some ceremonies; and these in religion, the ancienter they be the better, so [as long as] they may fit the time and place... And scarce anything hath hurt religion more in these broken times than an opinion in too many men, that because Rome had thrust some unnecessary and many superstitious ceremonies upon the Church, therefore the Reformation must have none at all; not considering therewhile, that ceremonies are the hedge that fence the substance of religion from all the indignities which profaneness and sacrilege too commonly put upon it.

*William Laud, in an open letter to Charles I, 'The Works of William Laud', quoted in Daniels and Morrill, **Charles I***

Logical though these ideas might be, to impose them on a worried nation was politically unwise; to argue that such imposition was the duty of the Bishops ('to whose place and function it doth properly belong, to give direction in that point' according to the Privy Council in 1633), inevitably brought them under attack. Yet the bishops were not the only focus of discontent, for it was clear that the new emphasis on authority and uniformity came from the king himself. Charles was determined to impose his own authority by enforcing existing rules, but his new orders went further. By reducing the scope for ministers to introduce spontaneous prayer or express their views through preaching, he intended to prevent the expression of any opposing or conflicting interpretations. In 1633 Charles and Laud issued instructions that afternoon sermons should be replaced by formal catechising and that no lecturers should be appointed to preach unless they were also prepared to carry out services and ceremonies as set out in the Prayer Book. This removed a popular device by which more strictly puritan ministers had been able to function in the Church without offence to their 'tender consciences'.

It must be said that these policies did attract some support, and were doing no more than Elizabeth had done in her time. What made the approach so dangerous was that it destroyed the existing compromise in the Church (established by James and Archbishop Abbot after 1611); worse, it was accompanied by clerical pretensions and a sympathy for Catholicism that Charles's predecessors had never displayed.

Catholicism and the Bishops

Neither Charles nor Laud was a Roman Catholic, but neither did they share the common Protestant view that the Pope was the Anti-Christ and the Roman faith a devilish mechanism used to corrupt true religion. Rather they regarded the Church of Rome as having lost its way and fallen into error from which it might one day be rescued. If this occurred, then unity might be restored; in the meanwhile the Anglican Church should regard it as a sister institution, to be helped where possible. In 1623 Charles had expressed such views in letters to the Pope as part of his attempt to secure a Spanish marriage. The same attitude was expressed by Laud when he stated that 'The Protestants did not get that name by protesting against the Church of Rome, but by protesting (and that when nothing else would serve) against her errors and superstitions. Do you but remove them from the Church of Rome, and our Protestation is ended, and the separation too . . .'

This attitude explains why Charles was prepared to accept the support of Catholics and why it was believed that he might well be in league with Irish and continental **Papists**. It explains why he allowed Henrietta Maria to practise her religion and to gain converts at Court. It also explains why he was unable to comprehend the fears that he engendered by these actions. To the more extreme Protestants and to the anti-Catholic majority in England he was failing in his duty as a Protestant monarch. What was worse, he was opening the way for

Papists to creep secretly back into the Church to renew their work of corruption.

Even those who did not share these concerns were likely to be offended by another aspect of Charles's beliefs – the enhanced role and status of the clergy and of the bishops in particular. The view that the Roman Church had been originally valid but had fallen into error allowed the Bishops to trace their descent from the early Christians and to restore the doctrine of **Apostolic succession**. This meant that the original authority given by Christ to his apostles had been passed down through the Church of Rome and then through its Anglican successor. Bishops, and the clergy they ordained, had an authority given direct from God. Although the king chose the person, their spiritual power was not dependent on his authority, and could not be removed. It was this idea that encouraged excessive pretensions among the Laudian Bishops – pretensions which infuriated many of the gentry and nobility both in and outside parliament. To make matters worse, Charles employed his bishops in secular politics, as Privy Councillors, Star Chamber judges and, in the case of Bishop Juxon, as Lord Treasurer. Such slighting of the traditional nobility by 'men of no name' who had gained power entirely through royal patronage, and dislike of clerical interference in secular affairs explains why the House of Commons were so determined to remove bishops from the Council and the Lords. It also explains why the Bishops Exclusion Bill was supported by later royalists as well as parliamentarians (see timeline on page 7).

KEY TERMS

'Papist' was an essentially abusive term for Roman Catholics, based more on their loyalty to the Pope than on details of doctrine. Papism, or Popery, indicated a loyalty to Rome, a foreign authority. It implied not only treason, but an association with a centre of evil. It was this prejudice and the unreasoning fears associated with it (similar in some ways to the extreme fear of communism that characterised the USA and western Europe in the 1950s) that dominated English political thinking throughout the seventeenth century.

Figure 7 A Puritan propaganda drawing showing 'Rattle-Head' (half William Laud and half the queen's catholic confessor) refusing the book offered by the Puritan, Sound-Head, but accepting the religious ornament offered by the monk, Round-Head.

Apostolic succession was the belief that spiritual authority had been passed from Jesus himself to the Apostles (disciples) and thereafter through St Peter to the Popes and Bishops of the Christian Church. The key point was that this spiritual authority was independent of kings and parliaments. It had to pass through the Church of Rome, making it impossible to disown entirely the pre-Reformation church and what it represented.

Conclusion

It is clear that Charles did subscribe to ideas and beliefs that placed him at odds with many of his subjects, and that the most significant areas of conflict related to religion and the Church. It would also appear, however, that it was not merely a matter of beliefs, but of his determination to enforce them according to his own preferences that created conflict and eventually crisis. Charles had a clear vision of the society and kingdom that he wanted to rule, and a strong sense of his duty to work towards it. He was, as his admirers claimed, pious and sensitive, an appreciator of both beauty and morality. Unfortunately, in political terms his positive qualities were no great asset. Because he believed his vision to be right, and because he was a conscientious monarch, he could not comprehend opposition except as something motivated by malice and subversion. It may well be that his authoritarianism was increased by the desire to cover his doubts and uncertainties, as Carlton suggests in Source 7, and these conflicting pressures probably explain the inconsistencies that created the very damaging impression that Charles was not to be trusted.

Yet it is not enough to point just to the influence of his personality, because it was the interaction of that personality with his deeply-held convictions about kingship in state and church that made Charles a divisive influence and a danger to the constitution. Unlike Elizabeth and James, who had learned to temper their own preferences in the light of political reality, Charles pursued his objectives without concern for 'the art of the possible' or even for the unity of his kingdoms. In this sense Charles behaved not as a king, but as the leader of a faction; in the end, he led that faction into a civil war.

TASKS

This chapter contains little new information on events. Although the headings could be used to construct linear notes on Charles as an individual, it is intended to facilitate investigation of certain issues relating to the part played in these events by the king as an individual. The tasks below seek to enable you to develop your own views of the matter, through the sources.

Evaluation and interpretation of sources

Read the sources included in this chapter as directed below, and answer the questions that follow.

1 Read sources 1, 2 and 3.
   a How does source 1 define and justify the king's 'absolute' power?
   b The judgement in source 1 related to James I's 'imposition' of new customs duties on merchants. Does this judgement conflict with the definition of the king's powers in source 2?
   c Why does James refer to 'his' laws in source 3?
   d How far does Charles accept that a king's power should be restrained by the law?
   e Using all three sources in the context of your own knowledge, describe and define the power of the monarch in early seventeenth-century England.

2 Read source 4.
   a What evidence suggests that Charles believed that kings should govern within the law?
   b Using your knowledge of his attitudes and beliefs, explain what Charles meant by parliaments 'in their right constitution'.
   c What did he consider to be the value and purpose of parliaments?

3 Read source 5.
   a What did Charles see as the duties of a monarch?
   b What do you think was meant by his 'honour' in the context of the seventeenth century?
   c How might this influence his approach to government?

4 Read source 6.

  a Explain the meaning and implications of the following phrases:

    i 'the double obligation of Justice and Necessity';

    ii 'a conscience grounded upon suspicious conjectures';

    iii 'much more concerning sovereigns' promises'.

  b In the context of seventeenth-century attitudes and beliefs about kingship, explain why Sibthorpe claimed that subjects should obey, even where kings were unjust.

  c How widely would this argument be accepted?

5 Using all the sources that you have considered so far, and your own knowledge of events, how far would you consider Charles's actions in the matter of the forced loans to be:

  i unconstitutional;

  ii politically unwise?

6 Read sources 7 and 8.

  a In what ways does Clarendon's description of the king support the views of Carlton?

  b In what ways do the two sources differ?

  c Which do you consider to be the more reliable source?

7 Read source 9.

  a How does Laud justify the imposition of ceremonies and set prayers in the Church?

  b Why would these arguments appeal to a personality such as Charles?

  c What does Charles's determination to impose this order reveal about:

    i his personality;

    ii his political skills?

8 In the light of this evidence, evaluate the argument that Charles's character and beliefs made a clash with parliament inevitable.

CHAPTER TWO

THE FIRST TREMORS, 1625–9

Objectives

◢ To analyse the problems that Charles faced when he came to the throne, with reference to the European context in which he had to govern

◢ To outline events from 1625 to 1629, and to explain how the open breach of 1629 came about

◢ To assess the causes of this conflict, and Charles's part in creating it

◢ To address the effects of the conflict on further political development.

In 1628, only three years after Charles ascended to the throne, parliament petitioned that he should respect the rights and the liberties of his subjects. A year later they openly defied his orders to end their sitting, and passed three resolutions condemning Charles's religious and financial policies. Infuriated by their rebellious attitude, Charles arrested the ringleaders, dissolved parliament and determined not to call another for the foreseeable future. This open breach signified that the tense relationship of the preceding years had finally erupted into a serious clash. It marked the beginning of a slide into conflict, and ultimately war, within the governing elite.

The title of this chapter is derived from an article by Lawrence Stone ('The Results of the English Revolutions of the Seventeenth Century' in J. Pocock (ed.), *Three British Revolutions. 1641, 1688, 1776*) in which he compares the Civil Wars to an earthquake. Stone argues that the problems of 1628–9 provided a 'premonitory tremor' and the Glorious Revolution of 1688 an 'aftershock'. The analogy is useful in that it establishes a pattern of development and a relationship between complex events. It also implies that the seventeenth-century crisis was the inevitable result of deep-seated pressures and problems. Many historians would challenge such assumptions. They might argue instead that there was nothing inevitable about the crisis of the 1620s or the civil wars that followed a decade later. While accepting that Charles had inherited difficulties, they would suggest that such problems could have been dealt with separately and by negotiation rather than conflict. This argument places importance on the character and role of Charles I, and therefore gives rise to two questions:

◢ Did the factors that caused difficulties between Charles and his parliaments arise from serious structural weaknesses, or from a simple clash of personalities?

◢ Need these difficulties have led to an open breach by 1629?

In addition, it is necessary to consider the nature of the breach of 1628–9. If it arose from deep-seated problems, then the later crises and war were probably also the result of these problems, and to some degree inevitable. If this was not the case, then the causes of the civil war must lie in the events of Charles's reign, and it may well be that the breach of 1628–9 was important as part of this process. In short, it is necessary to consider whether the quarrels of 1625–9 should be seen as a symptom or a cause of the seventeenth-century crisis. Thus a third question may be formulated:

◢ Did these events create the conflict between King and Parliament that ended in war in 1642, or was such a conflict already inevitable?

This chapter addresses these issues in three sections.

Problems in Government

Historians' views of Charles I are inevitably influenced by his unique role in presiding over civil war in three kingdoms and losing his head as a result. For the most part he has been judged from an English, and more recently British, perspective. He has rarely been judged as a European monarch, facing problems which were common to many others across the continent. While some historians have raised the possibility that the civil wars in Britain were part of a wider European crisis, the implications of this concept in considering Charles and his aims have often been limited to the claim that he sought to establish an absolute monarchy on a European model.

The wider European context is relevant to the study of Charles in three ways. First, the problems that he was required to address as king were in some ways common across Europe, and were certainly affected by events there. Secondly, the solutions that he adopted were not unusual among contemporary rulers, but reflected a common and quite logical response. Thirdly, an awareness of this, and of the effects of these strategies elsewhere, influenced the response of many Englishmen to what Charles was doing, and may help to explain the fears and concerns that he aroused. The nature of the problems that he inherited have already been addressed in Part 1; the purpose here is to assess how serious they were when Charles inherited them, and whether a serious crisis was in some way inevitable. One way of doing this is by comparisons with other European states, where stresses and strains arising from similar problems did not lead to civil war and the execution of a king.

The economy, trade and social problems

There is no doubt that the seventeenth century was a period when governments across Europe were facing acute difficulties. It is no coincidence that rebellions and upheavals occurred in a number of states at this time. Apart from specific rebellions, peasant unrest and disorder was endemic across Europe. In England, many of the problems were linked to trade, and in particular to the wool trade which provided 90 per cent of English exports.

Rising population stimulated trade and created opportunity for those who could capitalise on rising prices. Overseas trade grew, if somewhat erratically, and stimulated investment in new land and methods of production. At the same time, however, there was hardship for those unable to adapt, and widespread complaints about enclosure reflected a loss of customary rights for many of the poorer classes. The result was increased reliance on erratic and seasonal employment, and a social instability that no government could ignore.

In the 1620s England was troubled by poor harvests and a depression in the cloth industry, arising from changes in demand that encouraged the production of lighter *'new draperies'* and adversely affected the older English woollens. In 1614, James had been persuaded to sanction an attempt to develop cloth manufacture in England, known as the Cokayne Project, in which the export of unfinished cloth would be replaced by that of the finished product. The result was disastrous, since English workers lacked the necessary skills, and the Dutch and Flemish markets were simply closed to English cloth of any kind. Although the attempt was quickly abandoned, the after-effects added to the problems generated by structural changes. Moreover, from 1618 onwards, English markets in Europe were inevitably affected by the Thirty Years' War. Nevertheless, these problems were not particularly bad in European terms. The rulers of France, Spain and Germany were beset by war, the costs of war, and physical damage to resources far more directly than in England.

KEY TERM

New Draperies were cloths dyed in bright colours and lighter than the heavy broadcloths traditionally produced in England, which were exported undyed.

Finance, religion and foreign policy

Inflation also created difficulties in government finance, complicated by war and a technological revolution in military tactics and equipment. Incessant warfare across Europe, arising from religious divisions and dynastic rivalries, led to major advances. Not only was war frequent, it was also increasingly expensive. Despite Queen Elizabeth's caution, the war with Spain from 1588 to 1604 undermined royal finances, and James had sought to avoid entanglement in European rivalries. Nevertheless, there were some factors that exerted a pressure for England to embark on an active foreign policy.

In the first place, England was the largest of the Protestant powers. Calls in parliament for both Elizabeth and James to intervene in Europe reflected a sense that England ought to play a leading role in the defence of Protestantism. Secondly, religious tensions and dynastic rivalries created a real threat that Catholic monarchs in Europe would launch an attack on protestant England. Again, both Elizabeth and James tried to counteract the threat without resorting to expensive wars, with varying levels of success. In 1618, however, these problems were significantly increased, with the outbreak of the Thirty Years' War.

Beginning in Germany, it represented the climax of sixteenth-century religious divisions and of the dynastic rivalry between France and the Spanish/Austrian Hapsburgs. Despite the fact that his daughter Elizabeth and her husband were driven from their lands in the German Palatinate by the Hapsburgs, James refused to become involved. He had tried instead to negotiate with Spain through a marriage between

Charles and the Infanta (the eldest daughter of the Spanish king). Parliament's fury at this pandering to Catholics was reinforced by Charles's anger when his suit was rejected. It directly influenced the early years of his reign.

There is no doubt that the war represented a re-assertion of Catholic power, which could seriously threaten European Protestantism and which stirred the anti-Catholic paranoia to which English opinion was always subject. It was inconceivable to English Protestants that their rulers could stand by and allow their co-religionists in Europe to be destroyed by the forces of evil.

The structure of government

It can therefore be argued that the situation in Europe at the time of Charles's accession posed a number of problems which demanded government action. However, to take military action in this context would require financial resources and administrative skills that the British monarchies did not possess at this point. The three kingdoms had widely differing legal and administrative systems. England was undoubtedly the wealthiest of them, but England was under-taxed and neither of Charles's predecessors had addressed the problem of resources with any significant success. Without parliamentary finance, English monarchs had little scope for action, and parliamentary finance would depend on harmony of purpose as well as mutual trust.

In grappling with these problems, the Stuarts were hampered by other difficulties. In the first place, they lacked a professional bureaucracy to execute their decisions. The Tudors had developed an effective structure for central government, but enforcement of their policies in the localities depended upon the unpaid services of the county elites as Lieutenants and JPs. While these officials could not shape government policy, they had considerable scope for inertia, passive resistance or simple inefficiency to blunt its effectiveness. The militia, for example – as Charles was to discover in 1639–40 – was totally unsuited to responding to any national military emergency. Similarly, the navy was barely worthy of the name, and piracy in both the English Channel and North Sea ran virtually unchecked. In 1616, Barbary pirates were able to inflict £20,000 worth of damage on the Newfoundland fishing fleet. In all aspects of government, it was difficult for Charles to operate effectively without the support and co-operation of the ruling class, in parliament and outside it.

An inevitable crisis?

There is no doubt, therefore, that Charles inherited important structural problems that had to be addressed. The likelihood was that any reforms would cause some tensions within the governing elite, as existing interests sought to defend their rights and privileges. This can be illustrated by comparable developments in Europe: in the France of Louis XIII and Richelieu, and in contemporary Spain. There, the growing power of the monarchy and policies of centralisation were leading towards absolutism. In Spain the centralising policies and increased taxation introduced by Olivares led to revolts in Catalonia, Naples and Portugal, while reaction to similar demands in France led to the Frondes (rebellions) in 1648–52. In Britain these tensions were complicated and heightened by the religious divisions that cut across all three kingdoms that Charles governed. Moreover, the association of European absolutism with the Catholic Church made his task more difficult. It could be argued that a crisis in England was inevitable because the government faced demands that could not be met without changes that the nation, or at least the ruling class, would find unacceptable.

There is, however, some evidence which contradicts this assumption. In many ways, England in the 1620s seemed to have avoided and dealt with the worst of the problems. The Elizabethan poor laws had helped to soften the effects of inflation and rising population, and Stuart England was free of the large-scale popular rebellions that had troubled the Tudors. Religious divisions had been softened by James's willingness to allow a measure of local variation in church organisation, and puritan ministers and their supporters had found it quite possible to live within the Anglican structure, however much they might wish for further reform. With gradual persuasion James had even brought the Anglican and Scottish churches into a similar framework, persuading the Scots to accept the restoration of bishops by 1621. He had broached the subject of introducing a new Prayer Book, similar to that used in England, but had dropped the idea in the face of determined Scottish resistance. The likelihood is that he would have proceeded slowly and by further persuasion to extend such uniformity when occasion allowed.

Even in the vexed area of royal finances, some progress had been made. Despite pressures, James had avoided the expense of war. Lionel Cranfield, Surveyor-General of the Customs, had embarked on a programme of financial reform, which led in 1620 to the balancing of income and expenditure for the first time in James's reign. The Crown was still in debt, but in this, as in many other areas of government, there is no reason to doubt that further progress could be made if problems were handled sensitively.

It can be said therefore, that Charles shared many of the problems facing European rulers at this time, that they were structural and serious, but that the final outcome would depend on how they were addressed. Government needed to become more efficient and better resourced, and religious quarrels both within and between states would require careful handling. The relationship between central and regional or local interests would need to be redefined. Yet none of these problems were insoluble, given trust, caution and goodwill. Much would therefore depend upon the personality and actions of the king who mounted the throne in 1625.

The reign of Charles I, 1625–9

War and diplomacy

When Charles ascended the throne in March 1625 he was apparently at one with the political nation. Since 1621 he had played an increasingly active part in government, and the Spanish War to which England was currently committed had been the policy of himself and Buckingham rather than an increasingly tired James I. The war was popular, and parliament had demonstrated its support by voting three subsidies to be collected in 1624–5 in order to fund it. Nevertheless, problems were already mounting beneath the surface, and to a considerable degree they were the responsibility of Charles himself.

The apparent unity over foreign policy actually disguised serious differences. To many MPs the Spanish War was a protestant crusade against an old enemy, to be fought mainly at sea. A naval war had echoes of Elizabethan glories, and was both affordable and potentially profitable. For Charles and Buckingham, however, the war was a matter of personal honour, following humiliation in Spain during their failed visit to arrange a dynastic marriage in 1623.

More seriously, Charles was determined to attack Spanish interests in Europe and, as a matter of honour and affection, to restore his sister Elizabeth to her estate. Thus the money provided by parliament had been overdrawn in order to equip a naval expedition to Cadiz and a land army sent under the command of a German mercenary, Count Mansfeld, to the Palatinate. Under equipped and badly organised, the army got no further than Flushing in the Netherlands, where it simply melted away during the winter of 1624–5 through illness and desertion.

In these circumstances, Charles's first parliament (which met in June 1625) was not ungenerous in voting two further subsidies, but there were already signs of strain. The traditional grant of tunnage and poundage to the king for life was delayed, possibly to control changes in rates of duty, but there is evidence to suggest that anger at the conduct of the war and the waste of parliamentary subsidies in the previous year was also a motivating factor. To Charles, the decision to grant him the duties for one year only was an insult.

Further problems were building up over the related issues of the king's marriage and his religious views. Faced with a war with Spain, Buckingham had negotiated a marriage for Charles with Henrietta Maria, sister of the king of France. What appeared to be a logical diplomatic move was complicated by the fact that she was a foreign Catholic and that the terms of the marriage treaty gave her the right to practise her religion in England. To make matters worse, Buckingham had also agreed to send English ships to help the French take control of the Huguenot (French Protestant) stronghold at La Rochelle. This aroused suspicion among MPs that foreign policy was being influenced by Catholic sympathies, which were reinforced by Charles's patronage of the Arminian movement in the Church of England.

Religion and the Church

In 1624 parliament had complained to King James about the writings of Richard Montague (an Arminian thinker and writer – see page 23) who had turned Arminian ideas into an attack on continental Protestantism and aligned the Anglican Church more closely to Catholicism. Upon Charles's accession, Montague restated his views in a pamphlet entitled '*Appello Caesarem*' and dedicated to King Charles. When the issue was raised again in the parliament of 1625, Charles replied by appointing Montague to the position of royal chaplain.

Montague's offence was to emphasise the catholic origins of the English Church. He argued that the Elizabethan settlement was not merely a convenient compromise, but represented the true inheritance of early christianity, stripped of the unnecessary superstitions invented by the Church of Rome, and validated by the instructions of Christ himself. The Church of Rome was therefore a sister church misled by error, as were the continental protestant congregations. This opened up the possibility of cordial relations with Catholicism and threatened any distinctive Protestant identity across Europe. It also implied that the authority exercised by the king and bishops had been passed down from Christ himself, and was therefore derived directly from God.

This meant that two important and related issues were involved in the apparent doctrinal debates. The first was that of authority within the Church. If Montague's claims were accepted, then decisions affecting the Church belonged to the king and the bishops alone, with no place for parliament, parish ministers or laity. Puritans would have to accept the existing arrangements as final, losing all hope of further purification and reform. Moreover, knowing that they had the king's sympathy, the Arminian writers pursued their aims by arguing in favour of high-flown claims to a Divine Right of Kings, in secular as well as religious affairs. This concept of authority – of the right to impose a decent and appropriate orderliness – could not have been better designed to appeal to the outlook and temperament of the new king. Nor could it have been more offensive, not only to those of puritan inclinations but also to parliament itself and to anyone who valued a measure of independence in their religious thinking.

The second issue arose from Arminianism's implied relationship with Catholicism. The two had a similarity in doctrine and practice which inflamed the anti-Catholic paranoia that had become part of English thinking in the years of Marian persecution and Elizabeth's struggles with Spain. The Catholic Church was seen as the centre of an international conspiracy, seeking to destroy true religion and establish political as well as religious tyranny. Even if the Arminians were not themselves secret Catholics, their ideas of church organisation, use of ceremonial and appeal to traditional authority might allow Catholic thinking to creep back into the English establishment. Puritan reformers were certainly in the minority, but any attempt to reform the Church on Arminian lines would frighten and offend a far wider spectrum of English protestants.

Tensions, conflicts and the development of the crisis

By July 1625, parliament's view of Charles had changed considerably. 'You cannot believe the alteration in the opinion of the world touching his Majesty', wrote the Earl of Kellie. Complaints in the Commons about Montague and in the Lords about the high-handedness of Buckingham began to increase. In frustration the king dissolved parliament in August. In October the raid on Cadiz ended in a fiasco, depriving Charles and Buckingham of both glory and the expected plunder of the Spanish bullion fleet. Faced with mounting expenses, Charles was forced to call a new parliament in February 1626.

He sought to ensure its smooth running by using Court influence to exclude those who had voiced criticism in earlier years, notably Sir Edward Coke and Sir Thomas Wentworth, whose dislike of Buckingham was well known. Their influence was simply replaced by the even more hostile leadership of Sir John Eliot, who concocted a plan to impeach Buckingham on charges of high treason. Within the House of Lords an alliance had developed between Buckingham's personal enemies and puritan sympathisers such as Lord Wharton, Lord Saye and Sele, and the Bishop of Lincoln, John Williams.

Faced with a real threat to his favourite, Charles went on the offensive. In March he warned the Commons that 'parliaments are altogether in my power for their calling, sitting and dissolution'; in May he chose to interpret attacks on Buckingham as insults against himself and briefly imprisoned Eliot and Sir Dudley Digges. In June he requested that parliament provide further subsidies, and extend the grant of customs revenue to life. When the Commons demanded the dismissal of Buckingham as the price of their cooperation, he simply dissolved parliament on 15 June. In what was clearly a premeditated strategy, Charles followed up the dissolution with a proclamation insisting on total conformity to his interpretation of the rules governing the Church, and a demand for a forced loan to replace his lost subsidies.

In the year that followed, the situation went from bad to worse. On the one hand, the king pursued his objectives with determined efficiency. Arminians were promoted in the Church (Laud became Bishop of Bath and Wells in 1626 and of London in 1628), the forced loan was successfully collected (producing well over £230,000 by autumn 1627) and refusers were conscripted into the armed forces or imprisoned. Further savings were made by billeting soldiers on the civilian population, without payment. In November 1627 the judges reluctantly supported the king's right to such levies in the Five Knights' Case and the Church reinforced the king's demands for obedience. It appeared that the king was able to impose his will despite resistance.

On the other hand, the foreign policy disasters multiplied. By 1627 the marriage treaty with France and Buckingham's diplomatic blunders had led to war with Louis XIII, England's most natural ally against Spain. Buckingham's expedition to relieve the Huguenots at La Rochelle in September had ended in humiliating failure. Charles's attempt to influence the struggle in Germany by subsidising a Danish army was costing £12,000 a month, without any appreciable benefit. No amount of forced loans could cover such expenses, and faced with a choice between parliament and defeat, Charles agreed to summon a new parliament in March 1628.

There is a good deal of evidence to suggest that, even now, the problems could have been resolved by negotiation and cooperation. The nation had seen what an angry king could do and achieve, and MPs who wished to moderate his policies had been reminded of the dangers of provocation. The king, though, had experienced the limits of his power, and was aware of what he could gain from parliament. With both Sir Edward Coke and Wentworth back in the Commons, there were some restraints on the more volatile Eliot, and a cautious strategy was adopted.

The complaints against Buckingham were set aside, and Wentworth persuaded the House to vote five subsidies to finance the war. At the same time, Coke and Eliot drew up a Petition of Right which laid down clear legal limits to the king's power and defined his recent actions as illegal. The subsidy bill was not to be presented to the Lords until the Petition was accepted, and it was clear to Charles that this was the price that he must pay for his money. The pill was made less bitter by the pretence that the petition was merely restating existing laws which the judges had misinterpreted. The need to swallow it was reinforced by further defeats in Germany and at La Rochelle. In June 1628 the king gave his assent to the Petition of Right, thereby giving it the force of law, and the subsidy bill resumed its progress to the Lords.

The apparent harmony restored by these events was shortlived. When the House of Commons began to prepare a bill to approve the king's levying of tunnage and poundage, Charles denied that such authorisation was necessary. This raised once more the old issue of impositions and some merchants refused to pay duties. More seriously, religion and the Church began to re-emerge as a major issue. Since 1625 Charles had steadily promoted Arminians and ignored or rejected ministers with Calvinist views. In June 1628 he prorogued parliament after Eliot had produced a remonstrance against the growth of Arminianism. In November he reissued the *Thirty-nine Articles*, defined according to his views, and forbade any other interpretation.

KEY TERM

The **Thirty-nine Articles** listed the essential points of the Anglican faith as defined in the Elizabethan Settlement of 1558–9. Many were open to more than one interpretation, and Elizabeth and James had both allowed a measure of variation in how they were applied. It was this policy that Charles was now reversing.

When parliament re-assembled in January 1629 there were difficulties almost from the start. The king was offended by the obvious pleasure taken in the removal of Buckingham (by assassination). The issue of customs duties was raised immediately and in February a Commons committee produced a deeply critical report on changes in the Church. In March, Charles summoned the House of Commons to the Lords, presumably intending to announce a further prorogation. Led by Eliot and with Denzil Holles and Benjamin Valentine holding the Speaker in his chair to prevent the House rising, the members passed the Three Resolutions – against Arminianism in the Church and against the levying and payment of tunnage and poundage without parliamentary consent. The same day, a furious king dissolved parliament and declared that another would not be summoned until 'our people shall see more clearly into our intentions and actions' and have 'a better understanding of us and themselves'.

The causes of crisis and the role of individuals

The events outlined above demonstrate that the crisis of 1629 was by no means inevitable, but arose from the actions and interaction of the individuals involved. Charles himself was very clear about the causes. In March 1629, he issued a declaration in which he sought 'Howsoever princes are not bound to give account of their actions but to God alone' to explain his dissolution of parliament and his intention to delay the calling of another. In it he claimed:

the House hath of late years endeavoured to extend their privileges, by setting up general committees for religion, for courts of justice, for trade and the like;...so as, where in former times the Knights and Burgesses were wont to communicate to the House such business as they brought from the countries; now there are so many chairs erected, to make inquiry upon all sorts of men, where complaints of all sorts are entertained, to the insufferable disturbance and scandal of justice and government...In these innovations...their drift was to break, by this means, through all respects and ligaments of government, and to erect a universal over-swaying power to themselves, which belongs only to us, and not to them...

Like later Whig historians, Charles believed that there was a conscious effort on the part of parliament to increase its power at the expense of his own. He was, in other words, the victim of an opposition conspiracy, motivated by ambition and a greed for power.

The parliamentary opposition

There is little evidence to support this belief in an opposition conspiracy; indeed the term 'opposition' is, in itself, somewhat misleading if it is interpreted as implying an organised and coherent group. MPs were not in any sense professional politicians, but members of the regional elites who were periodically sent to Westminster to represent the needs of their communities. Between parliaments they were unlikely to have contact with one another unless it arose through business or personal relationships, or unless they represented neighbouring areas.

Party, or factional, organisation was more likely to develop in the House of Lords, but the dominant figure in the Upper House at this time was Buckingham, the king's friend and confidant. There was a puritan faction – centred on Lord Wharton, Lord Saye and Sele and Lord Robert Spencer – who had cooperated with members of the Commons in asserting parliamentary rights against James I in 1621, but they were not of sufficient stature to counteract the power of Buckingham. At most they were capable of short-term alliances to achieve a specific purpose, for example with the Earl of Pembroke and his friends in 1626, to prevent the impeachment of Bristol.

Opposition in the Commons can perhaps best be examined by considering the three leading figures who dominated the events of the 1620s: Sir Edward Coke, Sir Thomas Wentworth and Sir John Eliot (see profiles). A comparison of their backgrounds, interests and attitudes may make it possible to discern any common factors, and hence to pick out the key motives of those who opposed Charles and his policies. Other opposition leaders – such as Pym, Holles and Hampden – were to be of greater importance in the later part of Charles's reign, but were at this time less significant figures. In a sense their experience of protest in the 1620s provided a formative experience which affected their actions in the later part of the reign.

Profiles
Sir Edward Coke
1552–1634

In many ways the senior figure in the commons, Coke had sat in several Elizabethan parliaments before becoming Solicitor General and Recorder of London in 1592, Speaker of the House of Commons in 1592–3 and Attorney General in 1593–4. In 1603 he was knighted by James I, becoming Chief Justice of the Common Pleas in 1606 and Chief Justice of the King's

Bench in 1613. In the same year he became a Privy Councillor. In 1616, however, he opposed the king's use of the royal prerogative in a case involving the Bishop of Coventry and was removed from his posts. Coke's main concern was to protect the independence of the judges, and hence of the law. He regained favour by marrying his daughter to Buckingham's brother and was recalled to the Council and sitting in the Star Chamber by 1620. In 1621 he took the lead in parliamentary attacks on James's foreign and financial policies and in asserting the Commons' right to free debate. With other parliamentary leaders he was arrested and imprisoned for nine months. In 1624 Coke led opposition to the Spanish marriage and monopolies, and was kept out of parliament by Charles in 1626. Returning in 1628, he bitterly attacked the forced loan, illegal taxation and Buckingham's influence, and was the main architect of the Petition of Right.

SIR JOHN ELIOT
1592–1632

Knighted in 1618, having been MP for St Germans since 1614, he was appointed Vice-Admiral of Devon in 1619, and was a strong supporter of the Spanish War. In 1625, however, he played a leading role in parliamentary attacks on Buckingham, demanding his impeachment for incompetence. He introduced a Remonstrance asserting parliament's right to question the king's advisers. Eliot was imprisoned in the Tower of London, but was released after parliament refused to transact further business without him. He also called for the enforcement of laws against Catholicism and held decidedly puritan views in religion. In 1627 he was again imprisoned for refusing to pay the forced loan, but was elected MP of Cornwall in 1628 and worked with Coke in preparing the Petition of Right. Eliot was volatile, but was an outstanding orator, which may have helped him to persuade the House of Commons to carry the Three Resolutions in 1629. For this action he was imprisoned, along with eight others, but refused to apologise and defended his actions in writing. He died in prison.

Sir Thomas Wentworth 1593–1641

Thomas Wentworth was knighted in 1611, sat as MP for Yorkshire from 1614 and became High Sheriff of the county in 1625. By that time he had a record of opposition to any extension of the royal prerogative, and was particularly critical of Buckingham's influence and inadequacies. In 1627 he was imprisoned for refusing to pay the forced loan, and supported the Petition of Right in 1628. With the death of Buckingham, however, Wentworth saw the opportunity for king and parliament to reconcile their differences, and used his influence for this purpose. He disliked puritan influences, and approved of the attempt to establish greater uniformity in the Church. In 1628 he became Viscount Wentworth and President of the Council of the North, and was made a Privy Councillor a year later. Thereafter he was one of Charles's leading advisers, an architect of the policy of 'Thorough' which was the label given to the establishment of efficient prerogative government in the 1630s. In 1632 he was appointed Lord Deputy of Ireland, where he governed with iron control from 1632 to 1639. Recalled in response to the Bishops' Wars in 1639 (and created Earl of Strafford in 1640), he advised Charles to call parliament in 1640, believing that anti-Scottish feeling could be used to rally support. Instead he found himself threatened with impeachment and finally hounded by an Act of Attainder. Throughout his career, Wentworth's hallmark was efficiency. The determination of the opposition in removing him was probably a sign of how much they feared his ability. He was beheaded on 12 May 1641.

It is perhaps significant that Eliot – the most extreme and radical of the three – was the only one to have strong religious views, which may account for his actions in the crisis of 1629. These religious views were common to some of the opposition supporters, notably Pym, Hampden and Holles, and others who were active in passing the Three Resolutions. Both Coke and Wentworth combined this period of 'opposition' with long careers in royal service, however, suggesting that they were reacting to specific issues and circumstances rather than developing an 'opposition' mentality. On the other hand, Coke was one of those most determined to limit parliamentary taxation, while the apparently more 'extreme' Pym had a greater appreciation of the need to finance government adequately.

It is clear that members' concerns varied considerably, which further weakens Charles's concept of an organised conspiracy. What most seem to have shared were three areas of concern – a determination to defend the role and rights of parliament, a belief that government had to act within the law and an intense dislike of the influence of the Duke of Buckingham. It seems that the opposition to Charles in this period was not motivated by a desire for parliamentary government, but by a desire for good government (in their terms). At no point did they attempt to shift executive power to parliament. No attempt was made to influence the king's choice of advisers, or to direct the making of policy, but where that policy was deemed to be dangerous, as in religion, or ineffective, as in foreign affairs, the Commons asserted a right to call those responsible to account.

It was natural that Charles should resist such attempts – indeed the cycle of parliamentary difficulties began with James in 1621. In the terms of his 1629 Declaration, however, he saw such demands as an attempt to usurp his power to govern, and responded to opposition with an aggressive insistence on his prerogative rights that went beyond the limits of the law. Perhaps significantly, the point at which opposition was most united and most widespread was in response to the forced loan of 1627. It was this willingness to override the law which led to the Petition of Right, and to new fears over tunnage and poundage, and it was essentially the rule of law that parliament sought to defend in this period.

The Tudor monarchs had established a concept of government by king-in-parliament in which the monarch exercised power but laid down its framework through parliamentary law, and the Henrician reformation had extended this to include the affairs of the Church as well as the State. Over the decades that followed, the growing literacy and wealth of the Commons had made them more able to assert their views and interests. The arguments of lawyers like Coke developed these precedents into a concept that England was governed by an 'ancient and fundamental' constitution, dating back, like the common law, to Anglo-Saxon times. This constitution set limits on royal power, and it was Charles's lack of respect for these limits that united much of the governing elite against him. The Commons sought to restrain the king's freedom of action and influence his decisions, not to take the decisions in his place.

Unfortunately, this distinction meant little to a king who was determined to exercise his authority in pursuit of his duty as he saw it, and who found himself obstructed in the process. Moreover, unlike James, Charles challenged his subjects' religious prejudices, and ignored their religious fears. In many ways these religious quarrels were separate from the constitutional issues that motivated Coke and Wentworth, but the two were brought together by Charles's insistence on asserting his authority in both areas.

The Three Resolutions of 1629 bracketed the apparently separate issues of unparliamentary taxation and changes in religion, because to their authors the resolutions reflected two sides of the same coin. Those who 'shall bring in innovation in religion, or by favour or countenance seek to extend or introduce Popery or Arminianism' and those who 'shall countenance or advise the taking and levying of the subsidies of Tonnage and Poundage, not being granted by Parliament . . . or . . . shall voluntarily yield or pay the said subsidies . . .' were both undermining the legal rights and liberties of England by supporting unfettered authority. By 1629, therefore, a number of divisive but separate issues involving religion, finance and the rule of law were becoming enmeshed around the single issue of authority and the king's determination to exercise it in his own terms. What can be seen to have occurred in the 1620s is not an attack on royal authority by a coherent opposition, but a deterioration of the relationship between king and parliament. Ultimately this brought into being an opposition group whose ideology was formed by the experience.

The roles of Buckingham and Charles

If the 'opposition' were not responsible for the crisis of 1629, and it was not the inevitable result of structural weaknesses, then its causes must surely lie with the individuals who were involved. Some historians have criticised those who led the Commons in this period for failing to appreciate the requirements of government in an inflationary age, but they had little encouragement to do so. Essentially, neither the king nor most MPs were capable of visualising the kind of partnership that effective government would increasingly require, and which would eventually develop through a century of conflict. It is clear that for the most part the opposition were reacting to events rather than directing them, and that their aims, certainly after 1626, were largely defensive. Control of the government, and hence the political initiative, lay with the king and his friend and favourite, the Duke of Buckingham.

Buckingham had come to prominence in 1616, when he replaced the disgraced Earl of Somerset as James I's Court favourite. His qualifications for this role were charm, good looks and an affable temperament. It is clear that James's attitude to Villiers was based on homosexual attraction, but whether this was either reciprocated or expressed physically is uncertain. The importance of the issue lies in explaining the nature of Buckingham's power and the resentment felt towards him by those who regarded themselves as better qualified to wield the political influence that Buckingham was able to exercise.

Firstly, Buckingham was financially both needy and greedy. Rising from relatively humble origins and having a large circle of family and friends to support, he was not prepared to allow James's new financial discipline to extend to himself. The sale of monopolies, and of honours and titles, was managed by Buckingham for his own purposes and continued to increase. Between 1616 and 1620, 563 new knighthoods were sold, as opposed to 501 in the previous 10 years.

Secondly, Buckingham offended the nobility who regarded themselves as the natural advisers to monarchy. His humble origins, his wealth and pride, his sale (and therefore devaluation) of honours and titles, and his increasing control of political influence and patronage were all offensive to the aristocratic factions who regarded government and politics as their natural arena.

The significance of this can only be appreciated if the role of the nobility in politics is understood. While seeking power and influence at Court, the Lords also played a vital role in parliament, both collectively as the senior House and individually as patrons of many members of the Commons. The focus of parliamentary history in this period tends to be the House of Commons, partly because so many issues involved finance which was accepted as an area in which the Commons took primacy. Nevertheless, much political influence was exercised by leaders in the Lords, who traditionally had helped the Crown to 'manage' the lower House. When these men refused to act in support of royal policy, or acted in opposition, as happened when Buckingham was pre-eminent in 1625–8, the ability of the government to maintain control was seriously undermined.

Nevertheless, it was not the personality of Buckingham alone which was crucial at this time, but his personality in combination with that of Charles. While James lived, Buckingham's power was diluted by other influences. James's political experience and awareness ensured that he remained in control of policy, most importantly of foreign policy and the maintenance of peace. Only when the alliance of Charles and Buckingham wrested power from James in 1624 did England embark on the disastrously expensive wars that brought financial and political problems into the open in 1625–8.

Charles's introduction of a more restrained and dignified Court, his emphasis on formality and on personal privacy made him less accessible than his father. Thus Buckingham's control of influence and patronage was made more complete. It was also natural that a young, inexperienced and uncertain king should rely more heavily on the advice of an older friend. This allowed Buckingham to pursue adventures in foreign policy that were intended to glorify both himself and his king. More seriously, however, it was Charles's reaction to these problems that made Buckingham's shortcomings so significant. By allowing Buckingham full control of military planning and expenditure, and by accepting his diplomatic manoeuvres over the French marriage, Charles surrendered his power to a man who was totally unfitted for it.

Even worse, when parliament tried to call Buckingham to account for his errors, Charles interpreted their actions as an attack on himself, and insisted upon a blind acceptance of his judgement and a willingness to pay for it. When he failed to achieve this, he deprived himself of legal taxes in order to protect his friend, and used his prerogative powers to force payments by other means. If Buckingham was a disaster, it was Charles who ensured that his errors created a political and constitutional crisis.

Moreover, it was the personality of Charles, not Buckingham, that introduced a further element into the crisis by entangling the separate and dangerous issue of religion in what were initially political and financial quarrels. However much it may have grieved him personally, Buckingham's assassination in 1628 provided an opportunity to heal the breach with parliament without loss of face. The Petition of Right had dealt with the legal problems arising from the forced loan, and parliament were willing to address the issue of tunnage and poundage in 1629. What really soured the atmosphere at this point was Charles's promotion of Arminians in the Church, and his total rejection of any puritan influence or argument.

In this area Buckingham had never played any particular part. Like his first patron, King James, Buckingham had encouraged and patronised ministers from several different factions in the Church, including puritan leaders like William Perkins and John Preston. It was Charles who identified himself exclusively with the Arminian faction, who made William Laud his chief religious spokesman, and who insisted on enforcing his personal interpretation of the Anglican settlement. In June 1628 Eliot introduced into the Commons a Remonstrance which criticised the growth of Arminian influence in the Church. In the following months Charles promoted eight new bishops, all of them Arminians, including Richard Montague whose views had caused such offence in parliament in 1624. Such actions could scarcely have been more insensitive or politically provocative, and played a major role in bringing the crisis to a head in March 1629.

It is clear, therefore, that individual personalities did play a significant part in creating the crisis of 1628–9, and that the most important of these was Charles. The errors of James I, the overweening influence and disastrous inefficiency of Buckingham, the naiveté and religious fears of some parliamentary leaders all played their part, but what brought them together was the king himself.

Conclusion

This chapter suggests that there was nothing inevitable or unavoidable about the crisis of 1629 and the open breach between King and Parliament that resulted from it. The underlying difficulties of financial weakness, administrative limitations and religious divisions had created tension between king and parliaments. They had raised issues concerning the extent of parliamentary rights and the correct balance of the constitution. While all agreed that government belonged to the king, that he carried out certain functions in and with parliaments, and that he should govern with respect for the law, the precise limits of his powers and how they should be exercised in particular circumstances created a number of grey areas in which different interpretations were possible. The demands of foreign policy and the influence of Buckingham brought some of these problems to a head. Charles dealt with them by asserting his will. His reaction to resistance or restraints created fears as to what he intended. He then compounded these by abandoning his father's compromise in the Church and imposing views that were seen by many as dangerously close to Catholicism. What was, for Charles, the fulfilment of his duty to govern was seen by others as an attack on their cherished rights and beliefs, and in March 1629 they came close to an act of rebellion. In turn, this confirmed Charles in his belief that parliament as an institution was unhelpful and irresponsible, and that a faction within it was seeking to challenge, if not destroy, his power. The result was the decision to govern for the foreseeable future without such burdensome distractions. What Charles failed to appreciate was that this experiment would, in itself, confirm the worst fears of those whom he governed. It may therefore be concluded that the events of 1628–9 were not the inevitable result of a deep-seated crisis of government, but that they did much to create one.

TASKS

Explaining why there was a crisis in 1628–9 involves first establishing what happened and how the crisis built up. One way of doing this is to establish a narrative of events and investigate how one event led to others, as in the outline provided in Part 1. On other occasions, it may be more useful to see events in terms of people's *actions*, because actions are the result of particular decisions and therefore arise from particular intentions and motives. By examining actions and considering the motives and intentions that lie behind them, we may be able to make a more detailed examination of why those actions were taken; and by considering how the actions of one party affected the actions of others, we may be able to build up a detailed understanding of how, and to some extent why, a particular event or outcome came about.

This chapter has suggested that the crisis of 1628–9 occurred because of a series of actions and reactions between king and parliament from 1625 onwards, which makes it particularly appropriate for this kind of investigation. Therefore, you should begin by establishing the sequence of actions that took place, and then attempt to consider how this process gradually created problems between them.

1a Re-read the relevant sections of this chapter, before constructing a flow chart to show how the actions of king and parliament from 1625 to 1629 brought about the Three Resolutions and the Dissolution of 1629.
 b Pick out the key actions, or turning-points in this process.
 c For each of these, explain:
   i what the action was intended to achieve;
   ii what its effects were;
   iii how this differed from what was intended.
 d Using this information, explain how king and parliament came to an open breach in 1629, when neither had intended it.

The process above explains *how* the crisis of 1629 occurred, but it does not entirely explain *why*. The way in which king and parliament saw each other's actions was influenced by their ideas and beliefs. Therefore, if we are to understand the causes and effect of particular actions, we have also to consider the ideas and beliefs that influenced both the actions, and the way that others reacted to them.

2 Re-read the extract from Charles I's Declaration of 1629 (page 65) and answer the following questions:

  a What does Charles see as the functions of a parliament?

  b What complaints does he make about the behaviour and intentions of recent parliaments?

  c What does he consider to have been the purpose of this behaviour?

  d Using your own knowledge of attitudes and events in this period, explain

   i how far his interpretation was correct;

   ii what this indicates about his own attitudes and beliefs.

3 Re-read the extracts from the Three Resolutions (page 70) and answer the following questions:

  a Why would anyone who encouraged 'Arminianism or Popery' be betraying English liberties?

  b Using your knowledge of the period, explain why these beliefs were treated as being the same.

  c Why was it regarded as betraying liberty to pay tunnage and poundage?

  d What does this suggest about the role and power of parliament?

  e Why did MPs feel so strongly about these issues that they were prepared to defy the king and risk the safety of parliament and of themselves?

4 How was it possible for both king and parliament to accuse the other of 'innovation' in 1629?

CHAPTER THREE

TYRANNY AND REFORM, 1629–40

Objectives

◢ To decide if the Personal Rule represented a new approach to government, or merely a different strategy for reform?

◢ To establish how close Charles I came to success

◢ To determine why he ultimately failed.

The period from 1629 to 1640, when Charles ruled without calling a parliament, has been viewed variously by both contemporaries and historians. In the eyes of Charles's opponents, and the Whig historians who followed them, it was the Eleven Years' Tyranny – the king's attempt to establish an absolute monarchy, doomed to fail in the face of progressive forces and the establishment of liberty. This view has been challenged by 'revisionists' such as Kevin Sharpe and others, who have argued that Charles in fact came remarkably close to success. Conrad Russell has pointed to the king's success in balancing his budget, and to the inability of those who opposed his policies in England to find effective ways of making their opposition felt in the absence of parliament. Had Charles not attempted to impose his vision of order and uniformity on Scotland, they argue, he could well have established it permanently in England. A similar view has been expressed by John Morrill; and John Adamson has gone so far as to suggest that with greater determination in 1639–40 Charles could in fact have defeated the Scots and sealed his triumph in all three kingdoms.

These arguments raise a number of questions about the nature of the personal rule and its ultimate failure. The first centres on what Charles was trying to achieve. Given the nature of the problems that he faced (as outlined in chapter 2), it could be argued that he was merely trying to reform and modernise an antiquated system of government. From 1625 to 1629 Charles saw at first hand the weaknesses of the English system, and contemporary European experience would indicate that centralisation and a more uniform system of administration were the obvious means of creating greater efficiency. Whether or not it might lead to absolute monarchy, the personal rule was therefore quite consistent with the aims that Charles had already established.

In this context, it could also be suggested that the dissolution of parliament in 1629 was not the prelude to absolutism but an act of exasperation in the face of parliamentary obstruction and irresponsibility. Having failed to establish effective government by working with parliament from 1625 to 1629, Charles simply sought to establish it without them. Therefore the 'personal rule' should be seen as a change of strategy rather than a change of purpose. If this is the case, it becomes necessary to examine the methods used and the response that they evoked in order to explain why such a worthy enterprise not only failed, but ended in crisis and ultimately in war.

The impact of dissolution, 1629–31

The 1629 dissolution of parliament was followed up by a number of arrests and a series of declarations. Nine MPs were arrested, although five were quickly released. Eliot, Holles and Benjamin Valentine were held in various prisons to avoid writs of *habeas corpus* (which would have secured their release) and finally brought to trial in 1630, after which they were imprisoned in the Tower of London. These events roused little shock or condemnation in the country. Charles's Declaration placed the blame squarely on the Commons, and there is no doubt that Eliot and others had gone too far. Holles was later released after apologising to the king; Eliot's incarceration and death from fever two years later were partly the result of his stubborn refusal to do likewise. It was only in the light of later events that he came to be portrayed as a martyr for liberty.

Nor was there any significant change in the structure or personnel of the government. After the death of Buckingham in 1628 Charles had appointed Wentworth to be President of the Council of the North, and a Privy Councillor. Although Laud was already Bishop of London, neither yet occupied a position of particular influence. A refusal by merchants to pay customs duties collapsed in the face of the king's insistence on his dues and the imprisonment of one of them, Richard Chambers. There is no evidence that Charles intended to dispense with parliament permanently, nor that public opinion believed him to be doing so. His claim after the dissolution that he would summon no more parliaments until people were able to see and understand more of his purposes suggests that what he desired was a parliament that would cooperate. He clearly believed that, given time to demonstrate the benefits of the reforms that he envisaged, he would be able to persuade or convince the political nation to provide it.

If this is accepted as a genuine expression of his views, then it is a strong indication that Charles I did not consciously aim at absolutism or the destruction of the existing constitution. It is possible that his declarations and promises to protect the subject's rightful liberties were intended as a cover for such intentions, but this seems unlikely. Since the promises were also accompanied by more challenging, and characteristic, assertions that he intended to protect his own rightful powers, and to provide 'good order' in the Church, there is no reason to regard his declarations as anything other than an affirmation of his views. He intended to provide good government in his own terms, and was convinced that this would eventually prove beneficial and acceptable to his subjects.

The King's government, 1631–7

The structure of government created by Charles during the Personal Rule provides the clearest evidence as to his vision and purpose. What emerges is a clear and characteristic pattern – based on order, hierarchy and uniformity – which can be demonstrated in the four areas of the royal Court, personnel and administration, finance and religion.

The royal Court

As the king's household, the Court was the centre of both politics and society, the core of government and the pinnacle of the social hierarchy. It was also the clearest expression of a monarch's personality and political vision. The Court of Elizabeth had been a mirror for Gloriana; that of James was relaxed, informal and slovenly; Charles intended that his Court should represent order, hierarchy and majesty. Based on the Spanish formality that he had seen and admired in Madrid in 1623, it adopted a high moral tone with both duelling and sexual licence specifically discouraged. In 1629 and 1631 Charles issued new instructions which regulated the behaviour of courtiers to the minutest detail.

Access to the monarch was strictly according to social rank, and the position of the nobility was elevated in every way possible. The sale of peerages was abandoned after Buckingham's death and prerogative courts such as the Star Chamber were instructed to find in favour of the nobility in cases where they were challenged by those of lower rank. In 1632, for example, the Earl of Suffolk was awarded huge damages in a case of 'undeferential behaviour'. The purpose was not so much to enhance the status of the nobility, but of the monarch who stood at their head.

Similar attention was paid to courtly ceremonial. The ceremonies attached to the Order of the Garter were reorganised by Charles himself and conducted away from the popular gaze, at Windsor. Charles was not the first monarch to seek to enhance majesty in this way, but where Henry VIII and Elizabeth had utilised royal spectacle to build up the popular image of the Crown, Charles maintained a privacy and inaccessibility which was politically disastrous. Court masques and plays, designed to enhance the image of monarchy, were conducted within the confines of the palace. The collection of paintings and patronage of artists like Anthony Van Dyck, all intended to emphasise the king's power and status (see Figures 8 and 9), were displayed to an exceedingly limited audience. Charles did have more grandiose plans – for example in the building of a huge new place at Whitehall – but these were never brought to fruition.

After Buckingham, Charles had no close companions other than his French Catholic wife. His closest advisers, such as Wentworth and Laud, were kept at a distance – in Wentworth's case literally, since he was Lord Deputy of Ireland for most of the period. His admiration of Spanish dignity and Italian art was mirrored in his enjoyment of the company in the later 1630s of George Con, the papal envoy who was formally received at Court in 1637. Ignoring the advice of William Laud, Charles had not only recognised the power and status of Rome, but taken into close companionship a man who was regarded by many of his subjects as the servant of Anti-Christ.

The nature of the Court is highly significant in understanding Charles's aims and in explaining his failure. The arrangements reflect his personality: reserved, private and unable to communicate with, or manage, the personalities around him. They illustrate Charles's vision

Figure 8 'Charles I and Henrietta Maria depart for the chase' by Daniel Myrtens, circa 1630–32

Figure 9 'Charles I à la chasse', by Anthony Van Dyck, 1635

of monarchy: aloof, remote, but providing good government through an orderly hierarchy headed by the monarch, whose benevolence, moral worth and organising powers justified the uniformity that he was entitled to impose. They also reflected and heightened the lack of awareness that made him unable to see that he was creating opposition, and therefore unable to prepare for it, or respond effectively when it emerged.

Personnel and administration

If the Court symbolised Charles's ideas on government, their practical impact was felt through his administrative measures and reforms. The hallmark of Charles's government was the direct influence of the king himself. Few structural changes were made, but the king's attention to detail and his determination to see his orders effectively carried out did have an invigorating effect. Precise instructions were issued to all office-holders. Judges were given clear instructions to be passed on to local justices, and the Prerogative Courts offered a swift response that compared well with the more cumbersome Common Law courts. The efficiency of Wentworth in the North and in Ireland was widely respected or resented, depending on whether the person involved had benefited or lost by it. Laud's tenure as Bishop of London and Archbishop of Canterbury ensured that local visitations were properly and regularly carried out and regulations enforced through the Church courts and the High Commission. The policy of 'Thorough' with which the period is associated meant precisely what it said.

The achievements of the regime can be illustrated by an examination of the Book (or rather books) of Orders issued in the early months of 1631. Essentially, they were a response to the social unrest generated by a depression in the cloth trade and bad harvests, which peaked in 1629–31. They were preceded in the 1620s by new instructions to JPs to suppress disorder, restrict the movement of grain and reduce its use in making beer rather than bread. However the growing influence of Laud in the Council led to the adoption of a more systematic approach. In January 1631 the Council issued 314 books of instructions to local governors, regarding the collection and use of poor rates, treatment of beggars, enforcement of existing laws, control of local markets, movement of goods and upkeep of roads and bridges. While most of the instructions were not new, their massive scope, attention to detail and the careful supervision exercised from the centre had an undoubted effect.

By 1635 some local protests were heard against aspects of the laws, but a pattern had been successfully established by which energetic central government could affect and improve the administration throughout the country.

◢ Source

The poor were better treated and better cared for than ever before. Grain stocks were better administered and waste was curtailed. The quality of local government was markedly improved and little doubt lingered as to the Council's ability to cause the king's writ to run into local parts with considerable authority . . . But it was unfortunate that the implementation of the Book of Orders was one of the few domestic successes in Caroline policy.

L. M. Hill, 'County Government in Caroline England, 1625–40', quoted in
Conrad Russell (ed.), **The Origins of the English Civil War** (OUP, 1991)

There were some problems. The county communities did not always take kindly to outside interference. In addition, it was too easy for the government to become embroiled in local rivalries and factions. The influence of Wentworth in Yorkshire, for example, blurred the distinction between local and national issues. So it was no coincidence that many of those who gathered around the rival Savile interest in south Yorkshire would support the opposition in 1640, including Sir John Hotham, who denied Charles entry to the arsenal of Hull in 1642.

There was also, inevitably, a limit to what the government could achieve with essentially amateur personnel in local government. Some measures – such as attempts to regulate wages – simply failed through lack of support by employers and JPs, who were often one and the same. For this reason the system needed to be managed with a sensitivity that recognised the power of local interests and ensured that these were balanced and respected. However well-meaning and paternalistic the government might be, it had to recognise the existing social structure and the power of the governing class at local level.

This was also reflected in government at the centre – the favouring of one party over another was politically dangerous if carried too far. Yet this was precisely the strategy that Charles used in order to carry out his reforms; by promoting men who could be relied upon to do his bidding and to share his view of what was required. The point should not be pressed too hard. Charles did allow contrary views to be expressed, and the number of office-holders who supported the opposition in 1640 is evidence that he did not exclude them for their opinions. The nobility, the traditional advisers to monarchy, were accorded their place and due. Nevertheless, the most influential personalities on the Council were men who had been brought to prominence by Charles because they shared his outlook. Worse still, many of them were either clerics or Catholics.

By 1632 the dominant personality was Laud. With Wentworth in Ireland and his chief rival, Lord Treasurer Weston, increasingly troubled by illness, Laud was able to establish overwhelming influence. In 1632 his protégé, Francis Windebanke, became Secretary of State and when Weston died in 1635, he was succeeded by Laud's nominee, Bishop Juxon. In 1634 Laud obtained the dismissal of the Chief Justice, Sir Robert Heath, for religious dissent. Laud's influence may have been beneficial in terms of efficiency, but it also helped to create a strong anti-clerical feeling in a country that had come to see government as the business of laymen. Combined with the presence of Catholics and the queen's influence at Court, this appeared to some to be laying the foundations of a Catholic absolutism similar to that being created by Louis XIII and Cardinal Richelieu in France.

In terms of administration and government personnel, Charles's vision of reform met with mixed fortunes. Efficiency was increased, and he was able to ensure that his policies were carried out to a considerable degree. Within the limited resources available to him, Charles improved the quality of government and strengthened the elements that he cherished – order, hierarchy and uniformity. Nevertheless, there were limits to his success, and more importantly, it was bought at the price of creating resentment within parts of the political nation, and a growing suspicion of his choice of men to carry them out.

Finance
If Charles's administrative reforms led to mixed results, the same could be said of his financial policies. On the one hand, he achieved spectac-

ular results. By 1635 Weston had succeeded in balancing the budget for current expenditure, and by 1637 the king's income had reached one million pounds a year – a 50 per cent increase on that which he had inherited in 1625. On the other hand, the measures taken to achieve this had created resentment, at least among certain groups. There has been considerable debate about the extent of such resentment, and of the resistance that was offered, because it is an issue that goes to the heart of Charles's chances of success. If he could guarantee an adequate revenue, then he would have no need to call a parliament until he was sure of its cooperation.

A variety of methods were used. In March 1629 the king issued a proclamation which asserted his right to continue to collect tunnage and poundage. In 1630, and again in 1635, he appointed a Commission for Defective Titles, which examined the title by which crown tenants held their land and agreed new terms for any who could not prove their rights. In addition, the commission negotiated payments from those who had illegally enclosed waste or common land, or had encroached on royal forests. In 1634 this last activity was also the subject of a special judicial enquiry. In 1630 a commission was appointed to compound with those who held land worth £40 a year and so were entitled to a knighthood, but had failed to take it up because of the costs involved. This device raised £165,000 between 1630 and 1635.

These measures exploited the king's ancient feudal rights. They fell mainly on the propertied classes. Suggestions that the government was attempting to serve the cause of social justice, for example by the fines for enclosure, are somewhat undermined by the fact that the enclosures were allowed to remain – the only effect was that the government profited from them. Similarly, proclamations to restrict new building around London may have been intended to control the growth of the city, but served mainly to bring in fines from those who were building and fees from tradesmen.

The most obvious examples of government greed and cynicism, however, arise from the renewed sale of monopolies. Not only did the practice reappear in spite of the 1624 Act, but Charles was quite capable of selling conflicting licences – for example, to the East India Company and to a rival association led by Sir William Courten. The most famous example of what Derek Hirst has called the government's 'moral bankruptcy' was the 'popish soap' monopoly. This was granted to a group of Catholic courtiers who fraudulently claimed to have invented a superior product. They even staged rigged demonstrations to 'prove' that it washed whiter.

By 1635 these measures had increased the king's income considerably, although much of the profit went to the courtiers and middlemen who made the necessary arrangements. Between 1631 and 1635, the crown's 'ordinary' revenue, which included the sources outlined above, averaged £618,376 a year. This was not, however, enough to guarantee financial independence – that possibility only arose as a result of the introduction of a new direct tax: ship-money.

In one sense, ship-money was not new. It had always been levied from coastal towns and ports as an occasional tax, particularly in times of war or national emergency, to pay for naval defence. Hence Charles's levying of the tax in 1634 – the proceeds of which were spent on the navy – raised few problems. What changed the situation was that in 1635 he repeated the levy, extending it from the coastal areas to the whole of the country. When the experiment was repeated in 1636, it became apparent that Charles was establishing a new annual tax, without the consent of parliament, which might well go a long way to removing his financial dependence on that body.

The issue of ship-money has been at the centre of debate about the strength and effectiveness of the Personal Rule. In the words of J. P. Kenyon, 'We are assured by Whig historians…that this aroused the most furious opposition in the provinces, and this "fact" is generally accepted. In fact, there is scarcely any hard evidence for it, and what there is associated with predictable individuals like the Earl of Warwick and Lord Saye and Sele [the leaders of the puritan faction]'. He goes on to point out that the money was used to equip a fleet to put down privateers in the English Channel, 'however ineffectually', and that there were few difficulties in collecting the tax until after the beginning of the Scottish crisis in 1637. In 1635 the government received all but £5,000 of the £199,000 demanded, in 1636 all but £7,000 and in 1637 all but £18,000. Only in 1638, when the assessment had been reduced to £70,000 by the government, was there a serious shortfall. Other historians, such as John Morrill, have supported some of these arguments. They point out that collection problems in 1638 and after may well have arisen partly because both government and JPs were preoccupied with preparations for the Scottish wars.

It is, however, possible to consider the issue from another angle. There was unlikely to be real resistance until it became apparent that the tax would be regularly levied – that is, in 1636. In that year there was one case of open resistance – the refusal to pay by John Hampden. When Hampden was brought to trial in 1637, the famous split decision of the judges in favour of the king – by seven to five – was not published until 1638. It is perhaps not surprising that many who disliked the tax chose to wait until the issue was clear before deciding how to react. A king who had been willing to imprison those who refused to pay a forced loan was not likely to act mercifully towards those who refused to pay an apparently legal tax. Refusal to pay was an extreme and potentially costly action, and the fact that it did not appear on any scale until 1638 does not preclude considerable and widespread opposition. Certainly the high yields obtained thus far were the result of immense and probably unsustainable care and attention from the Privy Council. It is probably impossible to be certain as to the extent of opposition, or whether Charles could have successfully imposed the tax on any long-term basis. However, the fact that by 1639, when the government's difficulties had made resistance a valid option, only £43,417 out of an assessment of £214,000 could be collected would seem to indicate a widespread dislike of the tax.

This argument is supported by the contemporary documents collected by Daniels and Morrill in *Charles I* (see 'Further reading' section). They include an account of the discussions among the Kentish gentry at the County Assizes in 1638, and their reactions to the king's success in the Hampden case. While there was a clear acceptance that the king must have money to pay for defence, there was an equally strong feeling that ship-money should not be used as a long-term method of raising revenue without the calling and approval of a parliament. Even more convincing is the opinion of the Earl of Clarendon, written years later as a royal adviser, that Charles had infringed the law and abused his power over the judges. Not only did this bring 'damage and mischief ... deserved reproach and infamy' to the Crown, but it also set a precedent of illegal proceedings which Clarendon declared to be partly responsible for the illegal and arbitrary behaviour of the Long Parliament. Coming from a royalist, this evidence does suggest that ship-money was both deeply unpopular and, in the longer term, dangerous to Charles and his crown.

It is clear that Charles's financial measures had improved the crown's position but not solved its financial problems. Moreover, the improvement had been achieved at a considerable political cost – measures were generally short term, hand to mouth, and often unpopular. It is this last point that is of most significance in assessing Charles's aims and chances of success. As Derek Hirst has pointed out, there were few genuinely new devices used. Most of the measures involved reviving or increasing old rights, using a kind of financial antiquarianism to extract maximum benefit from existing claims, rather than creating a new source of revenue such as the French monarchy's vast expansion and sale of offices and titles. There is little evidence of long-term vision or planning, which might have been expected in a conscious or coherent attempt to establish absolutism. The evidence provided by Charles's financial expedients strengthens the argument that he was not seeking to create a new monarchy, but to reform, strengthen and bring order to the one that he had inherited.

Religion and the Church

Enough has been said of Charles's religious views to indicate that this was also true in the case of religion and the Church. As we have already suggested, Charles was not a Catholic, but had a genuine devotion to the Church of England in which he had been brought up. His Arminian views and his choice of Laud as his religious spokesman represent a desire to raise the status and wealth of the Church and to create, through orderly uniformity, a new dignity and beauty in its services. The outlines of this policy were already clear enough by 1629 to create a hostile reaction in parliament, but in the 1630s, with the arrival of Laud as Archbishop of Canterbury, the king embarked on a campaign to ensure uniformity.

Unlike the earlier disputes, the focus of the campaign was not doctrinal, but directed at the organisation and practice of religion at parish level. In 1633 Laud issued new Instructions to the bishops, to be enforced throughout each diocese, on three lines of policy. The first was a reduction in both the quantity of preaching and the freedom with which preachers expressed their ideas. The second was a corresponding increase in the amount and importance of ceremonial and use of the sacraments, with uniform practice in all parishes. The third was the removal of communion tables from the centre of the church, among the congregation, to the traditional place of the altar, railed in at the east end of the central nave and approachable at most times only by the clergy (see Figures 10 and 11).

The significance of these measures lies in the attitudes that they represented. The emphasis on ceremony and sacrament rather than preaching and teaching was an attack on puritan ideas. It was intended to work through the emotions rather than the intellect, and to reduce debate. The practice of employing lecturers with a preaching function only, which allowed puritans to avoid participating in offensive ceremonies, was forbidden. Sermons were to be confined to morning and evening services, with the afternoon service used for catechising (the repetition of set prayers and learned responses). Extra meetings and classes for Bible study and discussion of its meaning were to cease. The religious thinking of the nation was to be controlled by an authoritarian Church in the service of an authoritarian king.

The placing of the altar at the eastern end of the church was expressed as a preference by Laud, but it was Charles who insisted on it. For him it was a matter of order and respect, but the issue caused fierce debate because of its implications. If the altar was railed off and approached only by the clergy, then this emphasised the status of the clergy as a separate order, above the laity. This in itself had Catholic associations, but it also recalled the Catholic mass. For many people, not only of the puritan faction, this was a return to superstition and idol-worship, attacking the heart of the Protestant faith. The matter was therefore controversial, and particularly obvious to the ordinary layman, who saw the physical evidence of the change in his own parish church. In 1637 even the Bishop of Lincoln, John Williams, was writing in protest against the change.

In some ways, Charles and Laud were pursuing reasonable objectives. Anti-clerical feeling had been strong in England ever since the

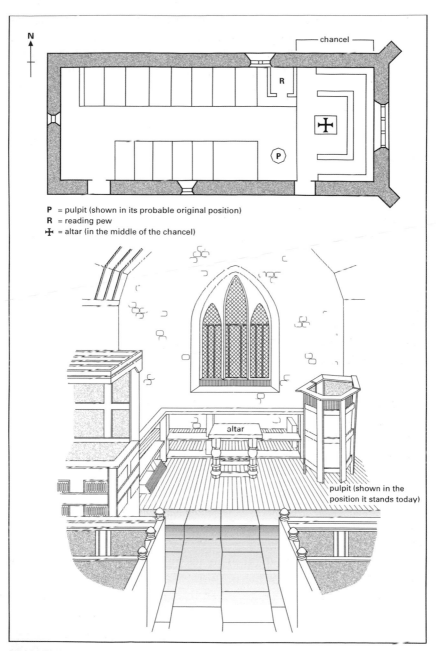

P = pulpit (shown in its probable original position)
R = reading pew
✠ = altar (in the middle of the chancel)

Figure 10 Modern drawing of the plan of Langley Chapel, Shropshire, built circa 1601 (*i.e.* pre William Laud)

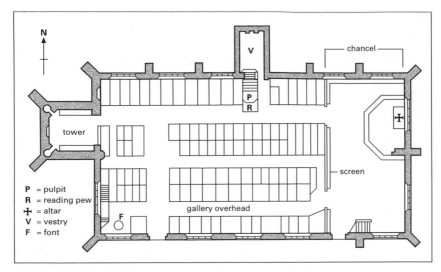

Figure 11 Modern drawing of the plan of St John's Church in Leeds, built 1634

Reformation, and the Church had suffered in both wealth and status. Many parishes were poorly served, standards of education among the clergy were patchy and variable, and the transfer of land from Church to laity through the dissolution of the monasteries had led to widespread *lay impropriation* of tithes and rights of presentation.

KEY TERM

Lay impropriation was the practice by which local gentry and borough corporations acquired the right to collect the tithes of a particular parish, and used this to control the appointment of the minister. In many cases they were able to select a minister and pay his salary. In some cases it was exploited for profit, leading to poorly paid and qualified clergy; in others it was used to influence the religious outlook of the minister appointed. Either way, it reduced the control that the king and bishops could exercise, and was therefore disliked by both.

What was, for Charles and Laud, an attempt to improve the quality of religious provision by creating uniform standards and raising the quality and status of the clergy, appeared to many laymen to be a renewal of the clerical pretensions associated with the Catholic Church. In this context, the presence of bishops on the Privy Council, the claims to derive their authority from the christian tradition, handed down from Christ himself, and the emphasis on authority and the special status of the clergy all came together to create fear of absolutism and catholicism.

These fears intensified as the period progressed. In 1633 Laud banned the Feoffees, a group of puritan gentry who had sought to buy up impropriations in order to provide good-quality ministers. Ironically, they were seeking the same result as Laud, but their choice of clergy and preference for lay control was unacceptable. When the judges found in Laud's favour, the impropriated parishes came to the king – to many, this was an attack on property rights as well as on puritanism. While puritan clergy found themselves forced to carry out offensive ceremonies, the Queen was permitted to practise the Catholic religion at Court, and to encourage converts. By 1636, Catholicism was becoming fashionable in some Court circles and the Pope's envoy, George Con, took up a permanent position at Court. The growing number of Catholics on the Privy Council appeared to be evidence of their power. Meanwhile, Laud used the power of both Church and State to enforce obedience and to silence opposition.

Control of the clergy was exercised through episcopal (bishop's) visitations and the Court of High Commission, which also imposed censorship through the licensing of books and pamphlets. When its powers proved insufficient, Laud turned to the Star Chamber. He used the power of the Privy Council in the case of Bastwick, Burton and Prynne in 1637. These three – a cleric, doctor and lawyer – had produced a number of pamphlets expressing puritan views, and finally attacked the influence of the Queen in an illegally published tract. They were accused of seditious libel, brought before the Star Chamber and sentenced to be pilloried, branded on the cheeks and to have their ears cropped (see Figure 12 overleaf). The sentences were carried out before a large and hostile crowd, which was shocked not only by the severity of the sentences, but also that they were inflicted on members of the gentry.

The significance of Charles's religious policies, therefore, goes well beyond purely religious issues. In themselves the reforms that Laud introduced in the Church would have offended puritans and their sympathisers, but these were never a majority of the population or even of the ruling classes. In addition, Laud's dominance of the

Figure 12 Cartoon printed in 1633 showing William Laud eating the ears of William Prynne, a Puritan who had been sentenced to have his ears cut off for criticising Laud's reforms.

Council and interference in affairs of state, his use of the secular courts to back up his religious policies, the elevated status and pretensions of the Laudian clergy, and his apparent attack on property rights, all combined to offend a much wider sector of the population. Most importantly, the similarities between Arminian and Catholic thinking, the presence of a catholic influence at Court, and the example of a catholic, absolutist monarchy in contemporary France all combined to raise the anti-Catholic fears which were endemic in seventeenth-century England.

What is also significant is the growing isolation of the king and his advisers. Charles's personal reserve and preference for domestic life combined with his ideas regarding the mystery of monarchy to lead him to withdraw from wider contacts into the company of a small group of like-minded associates. Thus he had little opportunity and less inclination to discover the views and feelings of his subjects, and to gain an understanding of what was politically possible. The result was that not only did he alienate many different factions and groups among his subjects, but also he was largely unaware of the extent of this alienation. Nowhere is this more clearly indicated than his decision to extend the programme of reform and uniformity into his northern kingdom of Scotland.

Assessment – Charles I, tyranny and reform

The nature of the Personal Rule suggests that Charles was not consciously seeking to restructure the government radically in order to establish absolutism on the continental model.

1 The Personal Rule involved little innovation in the machinery of government. Finance and administration were improved by more efficient use of existing methods. The most revolutionary of these was probably ship-money, but even this was an extension of an old device rather than the introduction of a new one. The social vision that seems to lie behind these measures was also essentially one of good order and uniformity within the existing structure. It involved the protection of the social hierarchy, paternal care for the lower orders, and preventing imbalance or disruption. Even in the Church, where his policies marked a significant departure from those of his predecessors, the changes were based upon a re-interpretation rather than a remaking of the existing rules and canons.

2 It is hard to believe that a deliberate attempt to create absolute monarchy could have been carried out with such limited political awareness. Charles's ignorance of the extent of discontent can be seen in his Scottish policy and in his continued belief that he could rally support behind it. Only after the fiasco of the Short Parliament in 1640 is there evidence that he recognised the need for concessions. His withdrawal into a highly-structured Court and failure to monitor the effects of his actions suggests that he was not conscious he was doing anything that required monitoring.

If these arguments are accepted, it then becomes necessary to define what Charles was trying to achieve. The indications lie in the nature of the reforms that he made. His personal rule was both the execution of his duty as king and an attempt to demonstrate its benefits. The prize was the willing cooperation of parliament, and the political nation that it represented, in preserving and maintaining the structure that he had put in place.

Charles did not, therefore, wish to destroy parliaments, but to confine them to their place as the supportive partner, enabling monarchy to function more effectively. On this basis, the criteria for judging Charles's chances of success relate to the possibility of convincing the majority of the political nation that his view of society was ultimately beneficial for them. On certain levels, these chances were good.

Although only a minority of thinkers, such as Sir Robert Filmer, shared his high notions of Divine Right, the governing class were well aware of their dependence on the monarch to guarantee their place in the hierarchy. Throughout the crisis years of 1640–42, 1647–9 and in 1659–60, the governing class showed their willingness to unite with the monarch when faced with the threat of disorder from below. Each of these crisis points also revealed their reliance on a single, national Church to hold society together and keep the lower orders in their place. If Charles had been able to exploit these fears and isolate his enemies through some judicious concessions, then he might well have been able to succeed in creating the religious and financial basis for a reformed monarchy.

Two factors prevented this outcome. The first was the existence of a significant religious minority who could not accept the changes made by Charles. For this religious minority, reform of the Church, or at least the reversal of Laud's reforms, was worth the risk of upheaval. The second factor was the personality of Charles himself. He was temperamentally incapable of understanding the fears that he engendered and the motives of those who thought differently. Hence he was incapable of making the right kind of concessions at the right time. It was therefore always likely that Charles would create a crisis of some kind, obliging him to recall parliament before his position was secure.

The Scottish rebellion and the end of the Personal Rule

By 1637 Charles appeared to have achieved many of his aims. The monarchy was solvent in terms of income and expenditure, although little had been done to reduce debts. Opposition to changes in the Church was muted, with little scope for expression, and the leaders of the puritan faction were considering emigration as their only way out. Perhaps most significant, a period of prolonged peace had benefited trade, so that revenue from customs duties had risen by more than 50 per cent, promising a possible route to long-term financial security. The situation was still finely balanced, and there is no doubt of the discontent felt by some, but Charles appeared to be in control of the situation.

Perhaps misled by this, Charles now determined to extend his policy of uniformity beyond the English borders – to Ireland, where Wentworth ruled with an iron grip, and to Scotland. Unlike his father, he had little understanding of the Scots; in some ways his hold on their loyalties was already uncertain. He had visited the country only once, in 1633, and tended to ignore the advice of the Scottish Privy Council, whose power he had systematically reduced. Instead he relied on a small group of Scots living in London, with the result that he was even more out of touch with Scottish opinion than with his English subjects.

Most importantly, Charles seriously underestimated both the Scots' desire to maintain their own identity and their loyalty to the Scottish Church (the Kirk). The Protestant reformation in Scotland had been thoroughly Calvinist, and had set up a presbyterian church of the kind that some puritans desired to see in England. It was not, therefore, surprising that Charles should seek to remove this uncomfortable example, as James had done before him. In 1621 James had persuaded the Scots to restore the office of bishop, but in an advisory role only, and had backed off in the face of fierce resistance to his attempt to introduce a set liturgy in the form of a Prayer Book. Worship in the Kirk generally consisted of sermons, Bible readings and improvised prayers. Lacking his father's tact, and his understanding of Scotland, Charles was determined to proceed more quickly and to introduce a revised version of the English Prayer Book.

In 1637 he ordered that the new Prayer Book should be read in Edinburgh churches (see page 25), imposing the order by proclamation and without reference to either the Scottish parliament or the Assembly of the Kirk. Infuriated by both the book and the manner in which it was imposed, the people of Edinburgh rioted. The Scottish Council withdrew the book while they considered what to do. Charles refused to make any concessions and in early 1638 the clergy and nobility, briefly united by their anger at such arbitrary English domination, met to draw up a Covenant (agreement) to defend the Kirk. Predictably, Charles was infuriated by their defiance, especially as the Covenanters claimed to be acting in God's name – so the stage was set for confrontation.

It was almost inevitable that the confrontation would be military. To Charles the Covenanters were rebels attacking his royal power as well as usurping his rightful function in deciding the religion of the state. To the Covenanters Charles was working for the cause of Anti-Christ, whether willingly or not, by accepting Catholics at Court and catholic ceremonies in the Church. Military preparations were further complicated by factions and intrigues, both in Scotland and at Whitehall. The quality of the English forces is indicated by Charles's choice of commander, the Earl of Arundel, on the basis that he was the senior English peer. Many of the gentry and nobility ignored his summons to fight, the half-trained militia were reluctant to move north, and when they did, many showed their real feelings by attacking church ornaments and helping local rioters to pull down enclosures. Even Charles recognised the weakness of his position and signed the Treaty of Berwick, allowing the Scots to decide on their own religious settlement. In the same year, 1639, a Scottish Assembly abolished both the Prayer Book and the Scottish bishops.

In fact, Charles had no intention of accepting this; the Treaty of Berwick was no more than a truce in his eyes. He was already preparing for further war. The fragility of his achievements in the Personal Rule was revealed by the refusal of London merchants to lend him the necessary money, and there is evidence that some of the English nobility were already in contact with their Scottish counterparts. In these desperate straits, Charles turned to the strongest personality among his advisers: Wentworth was recalled from Ireland, created Earl of Strafford, and allowed to take charge of the situation.

His advice was to call a parliament, hoping that traditional anti-Scottish feeling would enable the king to rally support. This may have been possible, although the flood of petitions that accompanied MPs to Westminster in April 1640 suggests that anti-government sentiment was running more strongly than Strafford realised. If so, Charles's tactlessness in demanding money without offering any concessions ensured that the possibility rapidly disappeared. The result was a chaotic session, in which some kind of opposition organisation began to take shape. In the Commons it was centred upon John Pym. In the Lords the leading figures were Pym's patron, the Duke of Bedford, with Lord Saye and Sele whose son, Nathaniel Fiennes, was already in touch with the Scottish army. It may well have been awareness that his enemies in England and Scotland were working together that pushed Charles into a hasty dissolution of parliament in early May, giving rise to its nickname of the 'Short Parliament'.

By now, the logic of events was moving quickly towards bringing the crisis to a head. Determined to assert his authority, Charles sought to raise a new army. In the process he revealed his continued failure to understand political reality by borrowing from English Catholics and appointing Catholic officers. Some of the militia sent to serve him busied themselves in burning altar rails and other Catholic symbols. Not surprisingly, the under-equipped English army proved unable to match the Scots, who had entered England by now. After a brief battle at Newburn-on-Tyne it melted away, leaving the Scots in control of Newcastle and able to force their terms on the king once more.

The Treaty of Ripon was signed in October 1640, by which time Charles had already conceded the need to call a new parliament. Its terms – a further truce, payment by Charles of their expenses at £850 a day and the postponement of further negotiations until parliament met – were designed to give that parliament the whip hand. Charles was facing opposition in both countries who shared overlapping, if not common, aims and who were working together to achieve them.

Conclusion – the failure of the Personal Rule

The speed with which Charles's government collapsed after 1638 has led some historians to regard it as inevitable, and to argue that the apparent success achieved up to 1637 was built on foundations that were too fragile to last. This argument is far from proven. Charles had certainly made inroads into some of the difficulties that he faced and he had done enough to demonstrate that the monarchy's problems were not insoluble. His methods created opposition, but until external forces brought about new pressure, those in England who opposed his ideas had little opportunity to challenge them. There is nothing to suggest that the regime faced imminent collapse from internal difficulties.

There is, however, evidence to suggest that discontent was mounting by 1637, and that the puritan faction had sufficient determination to maintain resistance of some kind. It is therefore likely that Charles had alienated sufficient elements in society to make it impossible for him to achieve his aim of convincing the political nation to be willing partners in his enterprise. This appears to be the case regarding ship-money, and was certainly the case in relation to the Church. The Long Parliament which assembled in November 1640 was unable to agree on a reformed Church, but the members were remarkably united in reversing the changes introduced by Laud.

What is more surprising is that Charles's experiment in personal government should fail completely, and collapse so quickly. The reasons for this lie in the Scottish crisis, created largely by Charles himself. To a considerable degree, the Scottish crisis encapsulates the whole range of problems that led up to the wider crisis of 1640. Its roots lay partly in religion, partly in the complexities of governing three separate kingdoms, and its outcome reflected the financial weakness of the crown. To that extent, it arose from structural problems facing the mid-seventeenth-century monarchy. Above all, however, it was caused and directed by the personality, convictions and love of uniformity that shaped Charles himself and drove him, perhaps inevitably, too far, too fast.

Examinations often include essays on the causes of the seventeenth-century crisis. They may vary in the way that they are phrased , but they all utilise the same material. It is therefore useful to establish a basic outline, which can be adapted to cover a variety of questions. Understanding the causes of the seventeenth-century crisis (remember that at this point we are talking about the crisis that came to a head in 1640, not the war that began in 1642) involves three essential steps:

- defining and explaining a number of factors (*e.g.* religious quarrels, financial problems) that worked together to create the crisis
- analysing how they worked together, and explaining what part each factor played in the process
- assessing which factors played the most important part.

1 Defining and explaining causal factors

It is useful to think in terms of factors, rather than people or events, because this will help you to organise your material in a sensible way, and avoid the trap of telling the story. A *factor* is essentially a group of events, actions and ideas, linked by a common theme – such as religion, king and parliament, or the personality of Charles I. The outline provided for you in Part 1 defined the causes of the crisis under five headings, which you may have used to organise your notes.

If you organise what you know into different factors, it becomes relatively easy to explain what each factor was, how it helped to cause the crisis and what part it played alongside other factors. Different factors do play different parts in causing something like the crisis of 1640 – some help to create a situation in which a crisis is possible, some build up to make it become likely, and others trigger it off. The first two groups tend to be considered *conditional* factors, creating the conditions that make it likely; the last groups are considered *contingent* factors, influencing the timing, shape and immediate impact of the event. Having identified different factors, you will need to consider which group they fall into.

Re-read chapters 2 and 3. Add to your notes any extra information that you have acquired about each of the five factors.

2a You can now begin to consider what part each factor played in causing the crisis. One of the best ways of doing this is to prepare some ideas, and then discuss them in a group. In group discussion, decide:

- ▲ which factors made a crisis possible in the seventeenth century
- ▲ which factors made it probable, or likely to happen
- ▲ which factors influenced when and how it happened
- ▲ Did any particular factor (or event) trigger it off ?

You can also refine these ideas further, and begin to consider which factors were most important, by discussing which factors had to be present for the crisis to occur, and were therefore necessary to it.

b In group discussion, take each factor in turn and consider how the situation would have changed if that factor was not present:

- ▲ Would there still have been a crisis?
- ▲ Would it have been as serious?
- ▲ Would it have happened at a different time?

Remember that you cannot be sure of your answers here, and do not need to be. The questions are only a device for considering how important a factor actually was.

3 You can use the ideas that you have developed through the above tasks to plan an explanation of the crisis of 1640, in which you show:

- ▲ what factors caused the crisis
- ▲ how they worked together
- ▲ and which factors were most important.

4 Finally, look back at Figures 8 and 9 on pages 81 and 82. How is Charles presented in these two portraits (and on the front cover)? What kind of image is created? Charles was actually a rather short man. Does he appear to be so in these portraits? How is the effect achieved? Why was this done?

CHAPTER FOUR

THE OUTBREAK OF WAR

Objectives

◢ To decide upon a definition of what is meant by the civil wars
◢ To establish why the crisis ended in war rather than compromise
◢ To assess the part played by events in the different kingdoms.

When the Long Parliament assembled in November 1640, war was not the expected outcome. As a result of the Scottish rebellion, the king was dependent upon parliament for financial survival, and the majority of MPs were agreed that their help would depend upon redress of the grievances that had accumulated during the Personal Rule. In the 18 months that followed, the attempt to gain satisfactory redress and to ensure security for the future led to a deterioration of relations between king and parliament, and to splits and divisions within parliament itself. These eventually led both sides to take up arms.

Recent studies of the period, especially the work of Conrad Russell and John Morrill, have pointed out that the civil wars were a British phenomenon, not confined to England, and commencing in 1638, not 1642. It was the rebellion in Scotland in 1638 that forced the recall of the English parliament; it was rebellion in Ireland in 1641 that brought the crisis to a head. War continued, moreover, until the English settlement of 1649 was imposed on Ireland and Scotland by the efforts of Cromwell and the Army, ending only with the defeat of Charles II at the head of a Scottish army at Worcester in September 1651. Explaining the outbreak of war therefore requires a definition of what is meant by the civil wars, and consideration of how events in different parts of Charles's three kingdoms interacted to create the situation.

Events fell into three phases. From 1637–40 it was Scottish affairs that dominated the situation as the king attempted to impose religious uniformity on his northern kingdom. This provided the opportunity for opposition in England to emerge, by forcing a recall of the English parliament. From 1640 to 1642 the focus shifts to Westminster. The power and resources of the English kingdom were by far the greatest of the three, and if Charles had been able to utilise them fully, he could probably have imposed his will in Scotland and Ireland. Hence the outcome of the struggle between Charles and the opposition in parliament was crucial for all three kingdoms. In this period the Irish rebellion helped to bring problems to a head, but it was the handling of these problems within England that led to a complete breakdown.

The final phase follows the outbreak of war in England, with Ireland and Scotland being drawn back into an English conflict. What this illustrates is that the three British kingdoms were inevitably inter-linked by their monarch, and that no settlement could endure in one unless accepted across all three. The end result, therefore, was that civil war continued until the rulers of England were able to impose their settlement across Britain as a whole. Ironically, it was Charles's attempt to do precisely this, by establishing religious uniformity in England, Scotland and Ireland, that initiated the collapse of authority and the military confrontation in the first place.

This interaction of the three kingdoms raises a number of issues which need to be addressed if the causes of civil war are to be understood. It is already clear that Scottish affairs, and the links between different religious factions in England and Scotland, played a significant part in bringing the crisis to a head. It is also necessary to consider why that crisis ended in war rather than compromise, and to assess the part played by events in the different kingdoms. Only then is it possible to consider the war and its effects, and draw conclusions as to whether it should be viewed as an English or a British civil war.

From crisis to war

The situation of November 1640 was unique in two ways. Firstly, the king's financial needs were so desperate that he would have to make some concessions. Secondly, he was faced with a coherent opposition group who had devised and agreed upon a clear programme of reform. This group, labelled by Conrad Russell as 'Pym's Junto', had long-standing personal and business links, but had formed as a group during the abortive Short Parliament of April 1640. When the early dissolution had prevented grievances from being addressed, they had turned to the Scots to provide a new opportunity. Thus, when they assembled at Westminster in November 1640, they had already formu-lated a political strategy.

Their plans fell into three parts:

- to obtain redress of past grievances and ensure the future security of parliament and the rule of law;
- to remove and punish the 'evil counsellors' who had misled the king and endangered the kingdom;
- to replace them with responsible ministers, preferably from their own ranks.

By the summer of 1641, most of this had been achieved. Laud had been imprisoned and impeached; his changes in the Church reversed. Strafford was attainted and executed, and the Prerogative Courts and ship-money abolished. The future calling of parliament was assured by the Triennial Act, which received the king's assent in February 1641. Over the next few months, however, the opposition made further demands:

- reform of the Church, removing the power of bishops;
- parliamentary control of the king's choice of ministers;
- control of the Army to be sent to quell rebellion in Ireland.

In so doing they alienated more moderate members, allowing the king to gather support. Ultimately, it was this division within parliament that allowed war to happen – without it the king would have been unable to raise effective forces. As it was, both parties took measures to defend themselves. Their mutual fear led both to take up arms and then the country drifted into civil war.

This process raises three questions:

- Why did an opposition who had achieved so much then undermine their success by pushing further demands, to the point of dividing the parliament on whose unity they depended?

- Why were some MPs, who shared the demand for redress of grievances, ultimately prepared to fight for a king whom many of them mistrusted?

- Why were these events allowed to drift to the point of a war that no one had wanted or foreseen?

The opposition campaign, 1640–41

Pym's Junto

The MPs who formed the opposition leadership were united by shared attitudes and assumptions. In the Commons the outstanding figure was John Pym, an experienced politician who had first entered parliament in 1620 and had been a supporter and associate of those, like Coke and Eliot, who had opposed Charles's high-handed methods in the crisis of 1628–9. He was ably supported by others, like John Hampden of ship-money fame, Denzil Holles who had helped to pass the Three Resolutions of 1629, and lawyers such as John Selden and Oliver St John who carried on the defence of the 'ancient and fundamental constitution' in the tradition of Sir Edward Coke.

Most of the group had strong religious views; some, like Nathaniel Fiennes who had maintained contact with the Scottish Covenanters, were in favour of a Presbyterian reorganisation of the Church. Behind these MPs stood a faction within the House of Lords – Fiennes's father, Lord Saye and Sele, and Pym's patron and employer, the Earl of Bedford, as well as the Earls of Warwick and Essex. In the 1630s, when no parliament was called, these men had maintained personal contacts and shared involvement in business ventures such as the Providence Island Company. But what really united them was their shared concern regarding the rule of law, the rights of parliament and puritan influence within the Church. The Short Parliament had enabled them to meet and to formulate their plans, which were carried forward in a series of secret meetings thereafter.

The parliamentary campaign

In November 1640 they had the opportunity to put them into effect. Clarendon later recalled a conversation with Pym in early November, in which Pym outlined the need to redress grievances and 'pull up the causes of them by the roots'. The speed and efficiency with which this process began shows clearly that this was a planned strategy. Parliament opened on 3 November with a speech by Pym outlining a 'papist' conspiracy in Church and State, and moving for a parliamentary committee to consider the state of the kingdom. This device allowed the committee to choose its own chairman, avoiding the control which the monarch could normally exercise through the Speaker.

On 8 November impeachment proceedings were begun against Strafford, and ten days later against Laud.

Meanwhile, the House of Commons listened sympathetically to petitions calling for the end of ship-money, abolition of the Prerogative Courts and reform of the Church; in early December they debated the Root and Branch Petition, calling for the abolition of bishops and reform on a presbyterian model. By late January 1641 Charles was forced to meet the Commons and appeal for financial aid. He indicated his willingness to accept reform, while warning of the dangers of disrupting normal government. In reply, parliament proceeded with a Triennial Act, to guarantee the calling of a parliament every three years. They presented it to the king in February. With ill-concealed resentment, he was forced to give his assent.

Thus far, the opposition campaign had met with complete success, but beneath the surface, there were already signs of difficulties to come. The Root and Branch debate had revealed a wide variety of views on the future of the Church. While there was general agreement on the reversal of Laud's policies, there was considerable doubt about what to put in their place. More seriously at this stage, the process of impeaching Strafford was causing problems. It involved his trial before the Lords on charges of treason brought by the Commons, but convincing evidence to support the charges was proving difficult to find. With the Earl showing every intention of mounting a robust defence, there was a real possibility that he would be acquitted.

In April 1641 the opposition abandoned the attempt to impeach Strafford, substituting instead an Act of Attainder, introduced by Sir Arthur Haselrig. This simply declared Strafford guilty of treason by Act of Parliament, avoiding the necessity of a trial. The problem, however, was that it would have to be passed by both the Commons and Lords, and receive the king's consent, which Charles had declared he would not give. Pym heightened the tension by revealing details of a plot by certain Army officers to free Strafford and forcibly dissolve parliament. He called on the help of supporters in London to facilitate the passage of the Bill. Despite some doubts, it passed the House of Commons, and with daily demonstrations by mobs of artisans and apprentices, the Lords were intimidated into following suit.

In order to pressurise the king, the opposition stirred up popular opinion by playing on fears of Catholic influence. By 10 May Pym had persuaded the Commons to sign a protestation to defend their rights against a popish conspiracy, and to pass an Act against any dissolution of parliament without its own consent. With the London mobs now threatening the Palace of Whitehall itself and in fear for the safety of his family, the king gave in. He consented both to the Act against Dissolution and the Attainder of Strafford, who was executed two days later, on 12 May.

The first turning-point: the death of Strafford

The campaign against Strafford changed the situation. While the opposition had achieved their objectives in the short term it was at the price of alienating some support, especially in the House of Lords. More seriously, it had been necessary to increase fears and tensions in the country as a whole. Most seriously of all, the king had been threatened, intimidated and humiliated. While there was no proof of his involvement in the Army plot, Charles's refusal to punish those who were, suggested that he had not ruled out violent measures. Already, the queen had contacted her brother, the King of France, to discuss the possibility of receiving aid. There can be no doubt that Strafford's death and the means by which it was achieved increased the likelihood that the king would turn to force as a means of solving his difficulties.

The opposition leaders could have no evidence of this as yet, but they would be aware of the possibilities. While parliament remained united and the king in need of money, they were safe, but if that situation were to change, then their cause, their lives and property would be in great danger. At the same time, their success confirmed their strategy of extracting concessions from the king by a combination of intimidation and pressure. They therefore pushed ahead with further measures. In July ship-money was declared illegal, and the Prerogative Courts were formally abolished. Most of the machinery which had made the Personal Rule effective had now been dismantled, and the advisers associated with it had been removed, but the process by which it had been achieved meant that redress of past grievances was no longer enough. What the opposition now needed was to ensure future security – for parliament, the rule of law and for themselves.

This was highlighted in June 1641, when the king announced his intention of visiting Scotland to secure final peace with the Covenanters. If he should succeed in removing his financial burden, then parliament's security was immediately in doubt. Even within the terms of the Act against Dissolution, the king could prorogue parliament and allow a lengthy gap between sessions, during which time the opposition leaders would undoubtedly be at risk. This was made more likely by a growing mood of weariness among many backbench MPs, who felt that their stay in London had been sufficiently prolonged, that most of their objectives had been achieved, and who longed to return to their estates.

Faced with these threats, the opposition leaders revealed their deep mistrust of the king and his intentions. In June they petitioned him to delay his Scottish visit and to consider ten propositions put forward by the Commons. These included a demand for parliament to approve the king's choice of advisers, and to oversee the protestant education of his children – conditions which Charles would undoubtedly find insulting as well as politically unacceptable. There is some evidence that he had considered an offer of government posts to members of the opposition, including the Earl of Bedford, with Pym as Chancellor of the Exchequer. The plan was prevented by Bedford's death in May, but might well have been accepted. What was now demanded, however, was a permanent commitment to seek parliament's approval of his chosen servants. It is not surprising that he rejected the demand, declaring that it would make him 'but the shadow of a king'. Perhaps more ominously, there were signs that a number of MPs, led by Edward Hyde and Lucius Carey (Lord Falkland), agreed with him. The opposition group were beginning to push their campaign further than some members would wish, undermining the unity of parliament. This was more dangerous because, at the same time, they began to turn their attention to the deeply divisive issue of religion.

Religion and reform of the Church

This was peculiarly complex, because opposition to Charles's religious settlement involved three overlapping strands. A minority of MPs and their supporters can be defined as puritans, committed to a radical, probably presbyterian, reform of the Church and the complete abolition of bishops. A much greater number disliked the power and pretensions of the Laudian bishops, particularly their role in secular (non-religious) politics and their power as members of the House of Lords. Beyond this, the vast majority in the country disliked the changes made by Laud and feared the growing influence and association with Catholics.

This spread of opinion was demonstrated in the religious bills and debates of May and June 1641. In May a Bill to remove bishops from the House of Lords (the Bishops' Exclusion Bill) passed the Commons, but in early June a combination of royal influence and the bishops themselves ensured that it was rejected by the Lords. According to Sir Henry Slingsby, 'This bred much murmuring in the City. The discourse of all men is they must now strike at Root and Branch.' Accordingly, a Bill was introduced into the Commons for the complete 'Root and Branch' abolition of the office of bishop, but met with such opposition that it had to be laid aside without a vote. This constituted a major defeat for the opposition. More importantly, it suggested that while there was widespread support for reducing or removing the bishops' influence in politics, their complete abolition and the destruction of their authority in the Church was a different matter.

The reasons for this are explained by Slingsby, who was firmly against such radical change.

◢ Source

I went with the Bill for their taking of [the Bishops'] votes in the House of Peers and for meddling with temporal [non-religious] affairs, but I was against the Bill for taking away the function and calling of Bishops... I could never be of that opinion that the government of the Church, as it is now established by Bishops and Archbishops to be of absolute necessity, so that the taking of them away should quite overturn the state and essence of the christian church; but I am of the opinion that the taking of them out of the Church... may be of dangerous consequence to the peace of the Church;... considering that this government hath continued from the Apostles... it were not safe to make alteration from so ancient a beginning.

*Sir Henry Slingsby in his **Diary***

For Slingsby, the issue of bishops was a political, rather than a religious, matter. In this he spoke for many in England. Unlike the king and Laud he did not accept that episcopacy was ordained by God, but unlike the Presbyterians he did not regard it as a dangerous legacy of Popery. Like many English gentlemen, Slingsby viewed the Church in terms of its political and social role, as a guarantee of good order in society and as a means of teaching the 'lower orders' the virtues of acceptance and obedience. It was not the place of bishops to interfere in government, but to remove their power and authority from the Church was to undermine authority itself, and to risk the greatest danger of all – upheaval from below.

In this sense Slingsby not only reveals why the Church was such a difficult issue for the opposition, but also shows a key source of royalism. For many of the opposition leaders, the bishops were a religious issue, a threat to salvation and the Protestant faith. They were therefore committed to the abolition of episcopacy, or at least its reduction to a symbolic or advisory role, and were prepared to take risks in pursuit of this essential goal. Many MPs, however, did not share these attitudes. For those, like Slingsby, who supported their political campaign to restrain the king and reduce the pretensions of the Laudians, such risks were unacceptable if they began to threaten the social order and their own place within it. An important source of royalist support therefore lay in the conservative outlook of those MPs who wanted to limit the king's power and assert the rule of law without reducing his capacity to preserve the existing order. If these objectives clashed, as they did over the Church, then the apparent unity of parliament could rapidly disappear.

By the summer of 1641, therefore, the opposition campaign had run into serious difficulties. Although (and partly because) they had achieved many of their objectives, it was becoming increasingly difficult to maintain the pressure on Charles that they believed was necessary to ensure complete success. In order to extract concessions from the king and enforce the redress of grievances, they were driven to use methods that placed themselves and their cause at risk. This led to heightened mistrust, and forced them to increase their demands and to encroach on the king's recognised and accepted prerogative powers. These demands, combined with genuine fears that their religious aims were too extreme, led to the first signs of real support for the king among moderate MPs. It therefore threatened the unity upon which the opposition campaign depended. When the king left for Scotland in August 1641, he left behind a situation close to stalemate and an opposition leadership beset by fears for their cause, their achievements so far and their own safety.

The emergence of the Royalists

The second turning-point: the Irish Rebellion

What broke the stalemate was the news, in October 1641, of rebellion in Ireland. The king's attempts to gain political advantage by building up support in Scotland had failed, although he had negotiated a peace that removed the financial burden of supporting a Scottish army. Before he had time to benefit from this, however, he was faced with the need to raise new forces to deal with Ireland. In this case there was no doubt of parliament's willingness to provide the means – the problem lay in the terms that might be imposed.

The impact of the Irish rebellion is hard to exaggerate in the context of 1641. In addition to the anti-Catholic paranoia which was part of English thinking at the time, the upheavals of the previous year and the wildly exaggerated rumours of Catholic atrocities against Protestant settlers in Ireland were enough to provoke hysteria. The reality was bad enough – perhaps 3,000 were murdered in the early days of the rebellion – but even the most inflated figures were easily believed. Rumours of an Irish Catholic army ready to land in England spread rapidly, and fears were reinforced by the king's slow reaction. Not until 17 November did Charles I return to England, by which time MPs were already considering the ways and costs of raising an army.

The king's slow response to the crisis fuelled opposition fears that he sympathised with the rebels. His Arminian beliefs, his Catholic wife, and his entertainment of Catholics at Court had already laid the basis of suspicion. Then on 4 November the Irish leader Phelim O'Neale publicly claimed to be acting on his orders. In the circumstances, it is not surprising that the opposition leaders dared not entrust the king with an army, yet they could hardly refuse to find the means of relieving their fellow protestants and dealing with the rebellion. Faced with such a dilemma they resorted to a strategy which was to divide parliament finally and ensure the emergence of a royalist party capable of fighting for the king.

The collapse of parliamentary unity

The first part of the strategy was to ensure parliamentary control of the army to be raised for Ireland. On 8 November, before the king had returned from Scotland, parliament offered to raise forces and Pym succeeded in attaching the condition that the king should employ 'only such councillors as should be approved by parliament'. Faced with resistance from the moderate royalist group led by Hyde, Pym embarked on the second strategy: to rally support in parliament by preparing a petition to summarise past grievances and outline those still to be dealt with.

In this Grand Remonstrance Pym recalled the problems of evil councillors and Catholic plotting that had misled the king, justifying the need to control the king's choice of advisers and remove the malign influence of bishops. As an attempt to unify parliament, it failed: it was passed by only 11 votes, thus revealing the growing divisions. Nevertheless the opposition pushed ahead, and on 22 November decided to publish the Grand Remonstrance in a direct appeal to popular opinion. On 7 December Sir Arthur Haselrig also proposed a Militia Bill by which an army would be raised for Ireland provided that its general should be appointed by parliament.

These actions provoked fury from both the king and his growing band of supporters. The Militia Bill was undeniably an encroachment on the king's powers, as well as a personal insult with its implied lack of trust. By publishing the Grand Remonstrance the opposition were taking politics to the people. Sir Edward Dering complained that, upon first hearing of the Remonstrance, he 'did not dream that we should remonstrate downward, tell stories to the people and talk of the King as a third person'. He was not only expressing outrage at the insult to the monarch, but deeply held royalist fears of allowing those outside the governing class to participate in politics and so threaten the stability of the existing order.

The open breach

In the days that followed, these fears were reinforced. Demonstrations in London were followed by elections to the city government on 22

December, in which opposition supporters took control. The king's response – the appointment of the brutal and unpopular Sir Thomas Lunsford as Warden of the Tower of London (in an attempt to overawe the citizens) – only provoked further demonstrations. At the end of the month these demonstrations kept the bishops from attending the Lords for several days, whereupon they demanded that all proceedings in their absence be declared illegal, raising the possibility of a backlash against their arrogance.

Throughout this period the king had watched opinion run in his favour and seen the opposition becoming increasingly isolated. Now the bishops' demands threatened to create new problems. At the same time, Pym had begun to float rumours of an attempt to impeach the queen. Infuriated by this presumption, and perhaps keen to act while his support was at a height, Charles decided to seize the initiative. On 4 January he appeared in the House of Commons, accompanied by 300 armed men, in an attempt to arrest five MPs and one member of the Lords, Lord Kimbolton (later the Earl of Manchester).

Few strategies could have been as disastrous. Not only was the king overriding the privileges of parliament, he was also showing himself as willing to take violent and arbitrary action. Had he succeeded in arresting the opposition leaders he might have been able to destroy the coherence of their support, and by putting them on trial for treason allowed Hyde and his party to take the initiative in parliament. As it was, the MPs had been warned and escaped into the City of London, leaving the king to protest the legality of his intentions to a shocked and angry House. His action would have been risky if it had succeeded – its failure was catastrophic.

The attempt to arrest the five MPs marks the beginning of the drift to war. Not only did it undermine months of patient work by Hyde and his party in presenting the opposition as the extremists, it also roused public opinion to a fever pitch. Uncommitted moderates swung back to the opposition, and the citizens of London vented their anger in further demonstrations. Claiming that he feared for the safety of his family, Charles left London on 9 January for Hampton Court. He later moved north to establish his Court in his northern capital of York. John Morrill has pointed out that this not only made further negotiations with parliament difficult, but by encouraging supporters to show their loyalty by joining him there, left the opposition a free hand at Westminster. In the weeks that followed, Pym obtained the exclusion of bishops from the Lords, and the passing of the Militia Bill in the form of a parliamentary ordinance, not requiring the king's consent.

This open breach between king and parliament brought the crisis to a head, but not yet to the brink of war. It was clear that the opposition campaign had failed in some of its key objectives, notably those regarding the Church, and that their efforts had resulted in the emergence of a significant royalist party. The motivations of the royalists varied. Some, like Sir Benjamin Rudyerd, had been concerned from an early stage to protect the effectiveness of government; while others, such as Hyde and Lord George Digby, had shown an early dislike of Scottish interference and links with the opposition. A greater number were motivated by affection for the existing Church, not in its Laudian form, but as established by Elizabeth. They intensely disliked puritan schemes for reform. In many ways these concerns overlapped, since Scottish influence did much to reinforce Presbyterian ideas among the opposition. In addition, some felt a traditional loyalty to the person of the king.

Most effective of all, however, in creating support for the king was a basic conservatism in the affairs of both Church and State. This created a deep fear of innovation, a sense that the opposition were pushing their demands too far, and that the lengths to which they were going would fatally undermine the existing order. It was this feeling to which Charles would appeal in the months that followed and which would eventually enable him to seek a military solution to his problems.

Charles I and the drift to war

Charles regains some freedom of action

In the months between the calling of the Long Parliament and the attempted arrest of the five MPs, Charles appears as a largely passive figure, unable to take decisive action because his opponents held the trump cards. This does not mean that he did nothing. When Strafford's death revealed the failure of his initial strategy and showed that a few, reluctant concessions would not secure the funding and support that he required, he looked for alternatives. His almost certain involvement in two Army Plots, the queen's overtures to France and his own attempt to build up a royalist base in Scotland, all show that Charles was willing to consider the use of force well before 1642. While he encouraged Hyde and the moderates to work for a compromise, he was also considering other methods of regaining control of the situation.

On one level this was damaging, serving to increase mistrust when evidence of his activities leaked out, or when he showed his hand as in January 1642. On another level, it is not entirely valid to criticise Charles on this basis. Throughout the period he made it clear that there were certain issues – notably his role as monarch and his religious views – which he regarded as fundamental and where he would not compromise. In addition, he regarded himself as a king threatened by potential rebels (who were almost certainly in contact with the rebels in Scotland) and therefore he had every right to deal with them by force if necessary. What prevented Charles from using force at an earlier stage in the crisis was simply his inability to rally sufficient support. Now that his enemies had not only driven him from his capital, but also created a backlash in his favour, he was able to pursue a much more active and coherent strategy in seeking to build up his support and power.

Both sides gradually took steps to secure their military position, although for the most part these measures were defensive. In January the king made a secret attempt to secure control of the port and royal arsenal at Hull, but was forestalled when parliament sent Sir John Hotham to act as military governor. Not wishing to create an open breach at this stage, Charles accepted the arrangement, but was furious when in April Hotham refused him access to the arms. By June both sides were moving to raise forces: the parliament calling on the militia while the king sent out commissions of array. Cromwell secured Cambridge Castle for parliament, while many individual royalists fortified their houses and castles for the king. Ultimately it was Charles who took the final step in August 1642, of raising his standard at Nottingham and calling for volunteers. By then the drift to war had already moved too far to be easily stopped.

The propaganda war

More interesting and more complex was the propaganda war that took place in these same months, as both sides vied for the support of the nation. The parliament's case remained as stated in the Grand Remonstrance – that the king had been misled by a papist conspiracy to destroy both Protestantism and liberty, and that it was the duty of parliament to establish sufficient limits and restraints to protect his true interests and those of the nation. The same argument was presented in the Nineteen Propositions of June 1642, whose rejection by the king was a foregone conclusion. The most startling developments in this field came from the king rather than parliament, indicating the extent to which he had recovered from the failures of the Personal Rule and the early months of the Long Parliament.

In December 1641, in a response to the Grand Remonstrance, Charles pointed out how many concessions and compromises he had made since 1640. Admitting a measure of fault prior to that year, he was able to distance himself from previous errors by using the parliament's own fiction of evil councillors. He was also able to raise fears of arbitrary government by pointing out the illegal actions of the opposition, and their use of public demonstrations to intimidate opponents. Finally, he was able to declare his unshakeable principles regarding the defence of law, the social order and the Anglican Church as established by the Elizabethan settlement.

Through the early months of 1642, these themes were reiterated with increasing effect. As John Morrill has pointed out, the English provinces saw a breakdown of authority as government at the centre weakened, with enclosure riots, political demonstrations and attacks on churches and church property. By June 1642 Sir John Hotham, who had played a key role in securing Hull for parliament, was expressing doubts about parliament's wisdom in continuing to oppose the king, 'lest the necessitous people' should use the opportunity to challenge authority and the existing social order. The collapse of episcopal authority resulting from the attack on the bishops led to the breakdown of censorship and the increasingly confident emergence of religious radicals. Their ideas were published in a flood of pamphlets and were spread by 'tub-thumping' lay preachers and at the open meetings of independent and sectarian congregations, especially in London.

Such social disruption enhanced the king's propaganda. He was able to assert the validity of Anglican authority and blame parliamentary schemes for reform for the 'irreverence of those many schismatics and separatists, wherewith of late this kingdom and this city abounds ... for the suppression of whom we require your timely aid and active assistance'. He was able to point to parliament's use of street demonstrations as responsible for the weakening of authority. Above all, he was able to identify monarchy with law, in protecting both the existing social order and the rights of subjects within it. Few arguments did more to gloss over the memories of potential tyranny.

It can be argued that by 1642 Charles had recovered a great deal of support, partly because of the failures and difficulties experienced by his opponents and partly because he was capable of exploiting these. There is no doubt that 1642 saw a drift back to the king, particularly among those who were motivated by political concerns. Lawrence Stone has argued that what enabled some to withstand the pressure for the ruling class to close ranks was religion. He points out that in Yorkshire over half of those among the gentry who supported parliament had puritan views, and almost one-third of royalist gentry were Roman Catholics.

Ultimately the gentry divided, with a greater number supporting the king. It is difficult to draw clear conclusions regarding the distribution of support and the motives behind it. All recent research has emphasised the complexities, the influence of local and strategic considerations, the reluctance to be involved and the prevalence of neutralism. In the end, those who willingly took sides were a minority. Nevertheless, within that minority, strong protestant views in religion were a major factor in maintaining parliamentary support, and fear for good order in society and in the Church was the strongest weapon to be exploited by the king.

The outbreak of the English Civil War

It is clear, therefore, that neither the outbreak of war nor the distribution of support was predictable in 1640. In November 1640 Charles was faced with a united parliament, demanding redress of grievances. Led by a clever and well-organised opposition group, parliament seized the initiative and the king could only agree, however reluctantly, to their demands. For several months he made concessions, but his obvious resentment and the methods that they had to adopt deprived the opposition of safety and security in their achievements. As a result they were forced into increasing their demands, creating difficulties in maintaining their support. They were, moreover, faced with serious problems in maintaining unity on religion.

The result was the emergence of a king's party who sought to establish a genuine compromise and gave Charles the ability to launch a counter-attack. He proved unable to use that support as the basis for settlement, largely because he did not share their desire for compromise. While prepared to make concessions as a tactical manoeuvre, he had no interest in compromise as a long-term solution. Hence he miscalculated and brought the situation to an open breach in January 1642. In those circumstances, however, he had certain assets. The nature of society and the fear of upheaval gave him significant support, as did the principles for which he determined to stand. The strength of his convictions, which had been a burden in seeking to reconcile differences, was a positive factor when it came to leading a crusade.

In the end, Charles was a major cause of war. This did not mean that he deliberately sought it, although there is little doubt that he felt justified in using force to deal with the situation. What makes him a factor in creating the war is that he lacked the ability to compromise, although he had the ability to lead. Unfortunately his personality and the nature of his convictions enabled him to lead one half of his subjects, while creating such fear among the remainder as to drive them into fighting against him.

A British civil war?

The war that began in August 1642 was an English (and Welsh) War. Charles was at peace with Scotland until 1643 when the Covenanters came to an agreement with the parliament. Ireland was in turmoil, but the rebels claimed to be loyal to the king. Nevertheless, it is clear that events outside England had played a significant part in creating the situation, that the opposition to Charles across three kingdoms shared common concerns and in some cases direct contact, and that any settlement would have to include agreement on Scottish and Irish issues. What is suggested by this is that the union of the Crowns of England and Scotland in 1603 had made governing both kingdoms more complex and initiated a new phase in the relationship between them.

James's accession to the English throne had ended centuries of royal rivalry, but had raised the question of how the separate kingdoms should relate to one another. His desire for union was resisted in both kingdoms because of political and cultural differences, as well as inequality of wealth and resources. The English feared that the Scots would be a drain on the Exchequer, the Scots feared English domination and the loss of their cultural identity. In these circumstances, James was wise enough to move slowly. Unfortunately, the same could not be said of Charles.

England, Scotland and Ireland up to 1641

Unlike his father, Charles was an English king by birth and outlook. This might have led to a conflict between the kingdoms anyway, had it not been for the religious divisions that characterised the period. Although the religious complexion of his kingdoms varied, all three were divided by the fundamental struggle between Protestant and Catholic that had dominated Europe since the 1520s. That struggle cut across any national boundaries, creating a more complex pattern of fears and loyalties. James I had recognised this, and sought to create a British uniformity that was both gradual and flexible. It was Charles, and his commitment to an Arminian (and English) uniformity, who brought these common problems to the surface.

Although Scottish resistance to these changes was heightened by their English flavour, the rebellion of 1637–8 and the Bishops' Wars that followed were first and foremost attempts to defend their religion. Initially, the Scots sought only to guarantee the safety of the Scottish Church and its presbyterian identity, which they achieved by their victory of 1639. It was Charles's refusal to accept this and his preparation for further war that led the Scots to establish contact with the English puritans in seeking a lasting settlement. Hence they insisted, after the king's defeat at Newburn, on the calling of an English parliament before a final peace was signed. This was not because they sought to control English affairs, but because it had become apparent that the safety of the Scottish Church depended on achieving a compatible settlement in England. By 1640 both the king and his opponents recognised that religious beliefs cut across state borders. They saw it as necessary to establish their preferred forms in both kingdoms.

Similarly, the Irish rebellion of 1641 was also a reaction to religious quarrels. The Irish and Old English Catholics were prepared to be loyal subjects, but only if their religious identity was respected. In 1625–8 Charles had agreed to allow a measure of protection to Catholicism in Ireland through an arrangement known as the Graces, in return for money and arms to help in his wars with Spain and France. Thereafter, however, these concessions had been eroded by Strafford. In the spring of 1641 the Irish had watched in mounting alarm as parliament involved itself in Irish affairs during Strafford's impeachment, with increasingly strong anti-Catholic assertions. The prospect of an agreement between the king, parliament and the Scottish Presbyterians, which appeared to be growing in the summer of 1641, provoked the Irish to seek the return of the Graces and the protection of their religion before any such agreement took place.

The outbreak and origins of the civil wars should indeed be seen in a British context. Both the king's desires and religious prejudices created a pressure for uniformity across three kingdoms. At the same time, religious beliefs cut across national boundaries, so that rivalries existed within, as well as between, the separate kingdoms. Hence the success of a settlement in one kingdom depended on the outcome of factional struggles in the others. In this situation, as Conrad Russell has pointed out, it is not surprising that upheaval should develop first on the peripheries, where government control was least secure. Thus events in Scotland undermined the king's position, allowing discontent in England to emerge and, by removing the strong hand of Strafford, eventually to allow Irish fears to erupt. It should also be pointed out, however, that what provoked this situation initially was the impatience, and errors of judgement, of Charles I.

The 'British dimension', 1641–2

What is more debatable is the importance of the British dimension in shaping the events that followed. From November 1640 the centre of developments was undoubtedly the English parliament, and its relationship with Charles. At that point, both sides aimed at a settlement, but failed to achieve it. Conrad Russell has argued that this failure was partly the result of Scottish intervention and influence. He suggests that it was Scottish desire to establish Presbyterianism in England that pushed the opposition leaders to demand 'Root and Branch' reform of the Church, thus dividing parliament. He has also argued that the royalist group that gathered around Hyde and Falkland was both Anglican and anti-Scottish. Finally, he has suggested that the failure to negotiate and avoid war in the spring of 1642 was partly the result of both sides looking to a Scottish alliance as an alternative.

In some ways, this argument is appealing. There is no doubt that the Scots were in contact with the opposition leaders from an early stage, and were in a position to demand some influence as the price of their support. It is also true that the Scots did wish to see a presbyterian settlement in England: they sought to achieve it in 1641, again in 1643 with the Solemn League and Covenant (the basis of their military alliance with parliament) and in 1648 as the price of aiding the king. This would also help to explain why the opposition leaders made the political error of introducing the Root and Branch Bill with the consequent loss of support.

Nevertheless, the point is not entirely convincing. In the first place, some of the opposition leaders had strong puritan views and would have supported a presbyterian settlement as a matter of conscience. Perhaps more significant was the desire to remove the power of the bishops and restrain the king's authority in religion. According to Sir Henry Slingsby, the determination to push for Root and Branch abolition of episcopacy came after the failure of the Bishops' Exclusion Bill, when it had become the only means of limiting their political authority. What is apparent after the death of Strafford is that the opposition leaders were well aware of the king's anger and his willingness to consider force, and that their only recourse was to remove the means by which he could exercise unrestrained power in Church and State.

It was therefore impossible for them to end their campaign at a point where parliament could have remained united.

This is reinforced by the undoubtedly genuine fear of Catholicism that influenced their plans and reactions, and the fact that they may well have believed that Charles had Catholic sympathies. This can be seen most clearly in their reaction to the Irish rebellion, and the risky strategy by which they sought to control the militia. It was this which finally divided parliament and gave the king the opportunity to rally support. The most logical explanation of the errors made by the opposition at this time is that they were genuinely fearful of a Catholic conspiracy, possibly with the king at its heart if not its head. Nevertheless, they were reacting less to the Irish than to the fear of wider Catholic influence, and the belief that Ireland could be used as a base for a more powerful Catholic assault.

These fears also explain the failure to negotiate seriously in the early months of 1642. Any settlement would require a measure of trust, and by 1642 this did not exist. The opposition had seen the Catholics rise in Ireland, claiming to have the king's support, and they had seen Charles take violent action against themselves. For his part, Charles had seen an organised campaign to force him to give up his rightful powers and an attack on the Church that he believed to be validated by God. For months he had been forced to make concessions that he did not believe to be justified. Both he and his family had been subjected to physical coercion and intimidated by mobs whom he believed to be organised and orchestrated by his opponents. As a king, Charles had every right to deal with rebels in whatever way he was able. It is not therefore surprising that his priority in the early months of 1642 was to use his opportunity to build up support, and that neither he, nor the opposition, were prepared to trust the possibility of settlement and enter serious negotiations.

Conclusion

What is suggested by these arguments is that the seventeenth-century crisis should certainly be seen in a British context, and that it consisted of British, rather than English, civil wars. However, the root causes of the crisis did not lie in the relationship between the different kingdoms, but in issues and divisions that cut across all three. The origins of civil war lay in political and religious tensions, and in Charles I's inability to deal with them successfully. It was this combination that ensured problems across three kingdoms rather than one. The significance of this lay in two areas. The first was that distance from the centre of affairs reduced the government's control, and that an initial breakdown was more likely because the king had three kingdoms to manage. The second was that, once a breakdown had occurred, the complexities of dealing with different factions in each of the kingdoms made a negotiated settlement more difficult, and contributed to the failure to find it. The British context did not cause civil war, but made it much more difficult to avoid.

Once war had begun, events in one kingdom could not be isolated and contained, and no secure settlement could be established if it was not accepted in all three. Thus it is not surprising that war spread beyond the borders of England, and that Scotland and Ireland were drawn into the English conflict in their turn. In 1643 parliament's need for allies led to an agreement with the Scottish Covenanters and to the involvement of sections of the Scottish nobility and the Highland clans in defending the king. Similarly, Charles's need to maximise his resources led him to conclude an agreement (the Irish Cessation) with the Irish rebels in 1644. This, in turn, confirmed the worst suspicions of the parliamentarians regarding his links with Catholicism.

When the first war ended in 1646, the English parliament tried to maintain their Scottish alliance and impose their power on Ireland, but the emergence of radical forces in England enabled the king to attract Scottish support and renew the war in 1648. When Charles was finally defeated and executed, it was recognised that the new English Republic could not be secure until its power had been imposed on Ireland (in 1649) and Scotland (in 1650–51). What the civil wars demonstrated was that the three British kingdoms did not, and could not, exist in isolation, and that the civil wars in Britain could only end with a British settlement.

TASKS

1 Explaining the outbreak of war

Explaining the causes of the civil war involves looking at long- and short-term factors; explaining the outbreak of war focuses specifically on how the crisis of 1640 developed into war in 1642. You will need a clear understanding of the process, and the part that different factors played.

a Read chapter 4 and make linear notes using the headings provided at the end of Part 1.

b Construct a flow chart to illustrate the process. Try to identify clear turning-points, particularly in relation to the growth of mistrust between king and parliament and the division of parliament into opposition supporters and royalists.

c Explain the part played in the process by each of the following factors:
- the king's financial problems;
- religion and the Church;
- events in Scotland and Ireland;
- the opposition leaders;
- the personality of Charles I.

You will probably find that these factors overlap, which will help you to analyse how they interacted. It may be useful to work in a group, investigating one factor each, and then comparing how often particular ideas or events appear in different reports. Consider:
- whether war would still have occurred in the absence of any factor;
- at what point war became unavoidable.

2 Testing ideas with evidence

One method by which historians approach the study of a period is to consider arguments put forward by other historians, and evaluate them in the light of the available evidence.

In chapter 1 you were able to study the character and personality of Charles I and to analyse contemporary sources in order to develop your own view of him. You have now considered the part he played in bringing about civil war in 1642, and your interpretation of that contemporary evidence can now be improved by a stronger awareness of the context in which it was written.

TASKS

In the extract below, Conrad Russell puts forward an interpretation of Charles's character, and of how he contributed to the outbreak of war. Using the evidence that was collected from sources 1–9 in chapter 1, you should now:

a summarise what Russell says;

b show how sources 1–9 support and challenge his arguments;

c use the results of the process to put forward your own view of how Charles, as an individual, contributed to the outbreak of civil war.

It seems fair to regard Charles I as a necessary condition of the Civil War. Without his decision to impose the Scottish Prayer Book, the whole train of events which led to the Civil War we know could not have been set in motion. A king without Charles's unusual ecclesiology [beliefs about the Church] would not have felt under nearly as much pressure to take that decision as Charles did. A king with a less clericalist view of the chain of command in the church would ... have taken more advice from the Scottish [Privy] Council and less from the Scottish Bishops ... Indeed, under a different king, many of these men would not have been Bishops.

A king less indifferent to evidence would have been a great deal readier for the uproar the Book in the event created, and might, in Machiavellian style, have been prepared with rather more force to quell a disturbance he would have foreseen. One may perhaps excuse Charles for imposing the Book, but it is much harder to excuse him for his surprise at the reaction he provoked ... In the course of the political storm the Scottish crisis created ... Charles's inability to read the political map meant, if nothing worse, that every decision was reached too late, and every attempt to calm feelings was made when they were already too aroused to be soothed.

Yet a comparison between 1642 and the relevant precedents [such as the depositions of Edward II and Richard II] suggests that we cannot explain the Civil War by saying Charles was incompetent. If that were all, either the English would have overcome their squeamishness about resistance and deposed him, or Charles would have ended up so destitute of a party that no war was possible ... It is here important that the depth of Charles's ideological commitment gave him skills as a party leader which matched his weaknesses as a national leader ... To say this is to say that Charles enjoyed an advantage over Edward II, Richard II and Henry VI because he ruled over a deeply divided society.

Conrad Russell **The Causes of the Civil War** (OUP, 1990)

CHAPTER FIVE

FROM WAR TO REVOLUTION

Objectives

◢ To decide whether the seventeenth-century crisis involved more than the personality and convictions of the king

◢ To determine whether his removal from the throne and execution were the logical outcomes.

In the summer of 1642, Charles declared war on parliament by raising his standard at Nottingham and calling for volunteers. Four years later he was forced to accept defeat, surrendered to the Scots and was later transferred to parliament's custody. Thereafter he entered negotiations for a settlement with both parliament and the Army leaders, while secretly negotiating for Scottish aid and a renewed civil war. When he was defeated for the second time in 1648, Charles found himself facing a determined minority who had concluded that, since Charles could not be trusted to maintain any agreement made with him, they had no alternative but to make a settlement without him. In January 1649 he was brought to trial, found guilty of treason and sentenced to death. He was beheaded outside the Banqueting House in his own Palace of Whitehall on 30 January 1649 (see Figure 13).

In 1642 neither Charles nor his enemies expected, or could even imagine, such an outcome. War was undertaken reluctantly, almost accidentally, with both sides turning to arms in self-defence. To a considerable extent, the forces that were capable of bringing about such revolutionary events emerged from the war itself – from the collapse of censorship which allowed radical groups and ideas to flourish, and from the need to pursue the war to victory which created a more determined military leadership. Nevertheless, it can be argued that the essential ingredients for the execution of the King, and the abolition of the monarchy that followed, were already in place. Although men were unable to see this at the time, the logical (but not inevitable) outcome of their interaction was the removal from the throne of Charles I.

Figure 13 Painting of the execution of Charles I, January 1649. The four small pictures show: (top left) Charles; (bottom left) Charles walking to his execution; (top right) the executioner holding up Charles's head; (bottom right) people dipping their handkerchiefs in his blood.

The conditions for crisis

It was always likely that the English monarchy would face a crisis of some kind during the seventeenth century. Conditions across Europe posed new problems for government and required the development of new methods and resources. Any foreign activity placed a strain upon the crown's finances and highlighted the inadequacy of its financial and administrative system. It was essential that this should be over-hauled (as it was during the struggle against Louis XIV after 1689) and it was highly likely that the process would cause tensions. In addition, the accession of James I resulted in a need to establish an effective rela-tionship between the different kingdoms of Britain, which was also highly unlikely to be accomplished without difficulty. In France and in Spain a similar process of centralisation and increased taxation led to mid-century rebellions; in each case the monarchy faced a threat to its survival in certain parts of their domains.

In neither case, however, did the crisis result in full-scale civil war and the deposition of the monarch. In Spain, King Philip IV made conces-sions to the rebels, abandoned his unpopular chief minister and restored his authority. Only in Portugal (an independent kingdom until the 1580s) and in the Protestant Netherlands was Spanish auth-ority successfully challenged. In France, the crown was able to separate the feudal nobility from their potential allies, and deal with each in turn. Essentially, the French rebels were motivated by self-interest and defence of their privileges. They lacked any unifying belief or ideology that could attract wider support.

The value of these European comparisons is two-fold. On the one hand, they reinforce the claim that Charles faced serious problems which were not of his making, by showing their common existence across Europe. They also highlight the unique factors present in the English situation alone, that made the crisis in Britain so serious. The first is the personality of the king himself – unwilling or unable to make timely concessions, driven by unbending principles and inca-pable of adapting to political reality. The second factor lies in the reli-gious beliefs of the puritan opposition, which provided an unifying ideology across classes, attracted wider support and gave individuals the courage and justification for defying their divinely anointed king.

The role of Charles I

There is no doubt that Charles as an individual played a crucial role in creating the seventeenth-century crisis. In 1625 he faced a difficult, but by no means impossible, task. His reliance on, and protection of, the inept Buckingham soured relations with parliament. His high-handed methods of raising money and lack of respect for the law brought matters to a crisis in 1628. Then his complete identification with an unpopular religious minority led to an open breach in 1629. His response was to dissolve parliament and govern without calling another.

This might have been successful had Charles learned to proceed more carefully, but driven by conviction rather than political reality, he pursued exactly the same objectives. Central supervision of local government was made more effective, money was raised without reference to parliament and the judges intimidated into declaring the measures legal. Unpopular ministers were placed in positions of influence, including clerics and Catholics who were regarded with fear and suspicion. Above all, the Arminian minority was given control of the Church, offending puritan beliefs and raising fears of a Catholic conspiracy. In these circumstances, Charles's apparent success by 1637 served only to encourage him to extend his strategy to Scotland, and so lead to the collapse of his personal rule.

The Scottish crisis and its aftermath revealed the full significance of Charles's character and beliefs. He had already shown a willingness to override the limits of law, and the conviction that, as a divinely appointed monarch, he was justified in doing so. However, his treatment of the Scots revealed the extent to which he could be blind to political reality. Not only did Charles embark on the imposition of religious uniformity against the advice of his Archbishop, but when faced with resistance he persisted in believing that it could be crushed by force. His attitude to the Short Parliament in demanding financial support without any redress of its grievances shows how little he understood the reality of his situation. Six months later, when forced to call another parliament, he had become aware that some concessions were needed but had little idea of how many, and how they could be effectively presented. His grudging acceptance of parliament's demands, accompanied by attempts to find alternative strategies through the Army Plots or French intervention, served only to increase mistrust and to heighten fears.

The same characteristics prevailed in the aftermath of his defeat in 1646. His opponents had assumed that there was a limit to Charles's determination – that he would ultimately accept the logic of defeat. This was not the case. While apparently considering the offers made by both Parliament and Army, Charles was looking for an alternative. In 1647 he fled to the Isle of Wight, from which he hoped to arrange French aid or rescue. In fact he was able to adopt an alternative strategy by encouraging unrest in England and a Scottish invasion. What he failed to realise was that he was now dealing with a different brand of opposition – in the end, the Army leaders were prepared to override parliament and the law in order to solve the problem of Charles I.

To a considerable extent, therefore, it was Charles himself who brought about the revolution of 1649. He had helped to create the crisis of 1640, and played a major part in unleashing war in 1642. He failed to recognise the changes brought about by that war, and pursued the same strategies in 1646–8 as he had done in 1640–42. What is also significant is that Charles's personal strengths contributed as much to his downfall as his weaknesses. Throughout his life Charles was guided by strong and genuine convictions. His conception of his role as king, his sense of duty to God and to his posterity and his deep religious convictions were at least as important as his authoritarian temperament in rendering him unable to compromise. Throughout negotiations with his opponents, he made minor concessions, but declared clearly that there were certain principles of government in Church and State that could not be altered. Given that his opponents were also guided by conviction, it is hard to believe that genuine compromise was ever possible.

The fundamental conflict

The implication of these arguments is that there was a fundamental conflict in seventeenth-century England which had to be resolved. It is here that the second factor – religion – becomes important. The conflict was essentially political. The rights of parliament and the rule of law played a crucial part in the evolving crisis, and continued to do so until real change was established in 1689. Nevertheless, it was religious beliefs that, at crucial moments, gave some the courage to take radical action. Again and again, as the crisis developed, it was those with strong puritan views who were prepared to challenge the king and to stand by their cause. In 1629 it was religious fears that sparked off the Three Resolutions; in 1642 it was those with strong puritan views who provided the core of parliamentary support and who felt justified in military action to defend the cause.

By 1649, the issues had changed. The emergence of religious radicalism had created a demand for religious toleration. It had driven many conservative puritans (including the Scottish Covenanters) into an alliance with monarchy. Nevertheless, it was again the determined religious minority who were prepared to take radical action to preserve their cause. In this case, it was the trial and execution of a king who had defied God himself by refusing to accept the verdict of battle. It was therefore God himself who justified such action.

Conflict, crisis and the role of the individual

It is clear that the seventeenth-century crisis in Britain arose from fundamentally different views of society, Church and State. What this determined was that there would be change, and that the process would involve tension and possible conflict. What determined that it would involve civil war and revolution was the character and personality of Charles I. Had Charles been merely inept, he could simply have been quietly replaced – as monarchs had been before. The problem was that Charles did represent one view of how society should evolve, and he was an effective party leader. Faced with the parliamentary campaign of 1640–42, he was able to spot his opponents' weaknesses, exploit fears of disorder and take his stand upon the law and constitution. He was therefore able to rally support and create a royalist party. Nor was he lacking in courage. Thus he would not give up his convictions, even in the face of defeat and the threat of death. Indeed, his behaviour in the winter of 1648–9 and his refusal to make any concession – even when Cromwell himself begged him to do so – suggests that he may by then have decided that martyrdom was his best option. If so, he was later proved correct.

By the manner of his death, Charles did much to restore respect for monarchy. His courage and dignity in the face of death, and his declarations that he died for law and justice in the face of military dictatorship, enabled royalist propaganda to associate monarchy with peace, order and legal government. The errors and excesses of the Interregnum that followed his execution also helped to reinforce this view. Hence, when the Army's determination to maintain a puritan republic finally crumbled in 1659, the monarchy was restored by overwhelming popular demand in the shape of Charles II.

This demand was so great, however, that the need to address the fundamental issues that gave rise to the crisis was ignored. The result was that, within a decade of the restoration of 1660, the old problems began to re-emerge. Suspicion that Charles II was a secret Catholic, that he harboured a desire for absolute power and sought to override the rights of parliament grew steadily through the 1670s. The open Catholicism of James, Duke of York and heir to the throne, brought these fears to the point of crisis in 1679. A clever, rearguard action by Charles enabled this crisis to be weathered, but the accession of James in 1685 brought it to the surface once more. When James made the mistake of challenging the Church as well as the parliamentary elite, he provoked the revolution of 1688 and the fundamental reform of the monarchy and its relationship with parliament.

The seventeenth-century crisis involved more than the personality and convictions of Charles I. Between 1625 and 1649 Charles did great damage to the monarchy, but his death and the difficulty of replacing him did much to restore its position. The re-emergence of the old divisions thereafter demonstrates that their roots lay deeper in society. The political and religious legacy of the sixteenth century required government to reform and evolve, either through an increasingly powerful and centralised monarchy, or through compromise with the governing elite in parliament. The personality and actions of Charles I, the precise combination of his talents, convictions and weaknesses, shaped this process through war and revolution.

FURTHER READING

The range of published material regarding the Crisis of the Seventeenth Century is vast. The following can do no more than suggest useful resources for those who wish to extend their knowledge and understanding, or to explore particular issues more fully. Those with an interest in the historiography of the period will find a brief outline of the different interpretations in Angela Anderson *The Civil Wars, 1640–49*, in the Access to History series (Hodder and Stoughton, 1995). A fuller coverage of the debates is provided in R. C. Richardson *The Debate on the English Revolution Revisited* (Routledge, 1991) which offers a full and thoughtful analysis of the issues. Those wishing to sample some of the classic interpretations should dip into: S. R. Gardiner *History of England, 1603–56*, William Haller *Rise of Puritanism* (Harper Torchbooks, 1957) and Christopher Hill *Century of Revolution* (Sphere Books, 1961):

The sixteenth-century legacy addressed in Part 1 can be more fully explored at a number of levels. Further information can be obtained from reference works such as the *Oxford History of Britain*, and John Morrill's *History of Tudor and Stuart Britain*. Others which address both sixteenth and seventeenth century developments are: A. G. R. Smith *The Emergence of a Nation State* (Addison Wesley Longman, 1984), Conrad Russell *The Crisis of Parliaments: English History, 1509–1660* (Oxford University Press, 1971) and R. Ashton *Reformation and Revolution, 1558–1660* (Paladin, 1985).

Works which address the wider European context are summarised in Richardson's *The Debate on the English Revolution Revisited*. Probably the most accessible is T. Aston (ed.) *Crisis in Europe, 1560–1660* (Routledge, 1965).

There are many useful, accesible books which address the seventeenth century in general such as:
Katharine Brice *The Early Stuarts* (Hodder and Stoughton, Access to History, 1994)
Roger Lockyer *The Early Stuarts* (Addison Wesley Longman, 1989)
Barry Coward *The Stuart Age: A History of England 1603–1714* (Addison Wesley Longman, 2nd ed. 1994)

Barry Coward *Stuart England, 1603–1714* (Addison Wesley Longman, 1997)

Derek Hirst *Authority and Conflict* (Edward Arnold, 1987) – a detailed account of events, 1603–58, which often clarifies incidents which other accounts have only briefly addressed.

The causes and outbreak of the war have been the subject of many different interpretations. Lawrence Stone's *Causes of the English Revolution* (Routledge, 1972) emphasises long-term factors:

R. Ashton *The English Civil War: Conservatism and Revolution 1603–40* (Weidenfeld and Nicolson, 1976) and Ann Hughes *The Causes of the English Civil War* (Macmillan, 1991) both address more immediate causes.

Anthony Fletcher *The Outbreak of the English Civil War* (Edward Arnold, 1981) provides an in-depth account of 1640–42.

The war in a British context is addressed by Conrad Russell and John Morrill. Russell's major work in recent years is *The Fall of the British Monarchies, 1637–42* (Oxford University Press, 1991), but both he and John Morrill have published a number of useful and accessible collections of essays. You should look especially for:

Conrad Russell *The Origins of the English Civil War* (Macmillan, 1973) and *Causes of the Civil War* (Oxford University Press, 1990)

John Morrill (ed.) *The Nature of the English Revolution* (Addison Wesley Longman, 1993), *The Impact of the English Civil War* (Collins and Brown, 1991) and *Reactions to the English Civil War* (Macmillan, 1982).

Morrill's work includes the effects of the war itself and other wider issues: information and further reading can be found in Anderson *The Civil Wars*.

The most extensive recent study of Charles as an individual is Charles Carlton *Charles I* (Routledge, 1981) which offers many interesting insights. See also the essay collections above, and a collection of documents and analytical exercises published by Daniels and Morrill for the Cambridge University Press in 1988, under the title *Charles I*. This contains a helpful bibliography which introduces you to related topics such as the nature of Laudian ideas.

INDEX

KEY TERMS

PROFILES

MAIN INDEX